The Computer Virus Crisis

The Computer Virus Crisis

Philip Fites

Peter Johnston

Martin Kratz

 VAN NOSTRAND REINHOLD
New York

Library of Congress Catalog Card Number 88-13496
ISBN 0-442-28532-9

Printed in the United States of America

Van Nostrand Reinhold
115 Fifth Avenue
New York, New York 10003

Van Nostrand Reinhold International Company Limited
11 New Fetter Lane
London EC4P 4EE, England

Van Nostrand Reinhold
480 La Trobe Street
Melbourne, Victoria 3000, Australia

Nelson Canada
1120 Birchmount Road
Scarborough, Ontario M1K 5G4, Canada

16 15 14 13 12 11 10 9 8 7 6 5 4 3

Library of Congress Cataloging in Publication Data

Fites, Philip E.
    The computer virus crisis / Philip Fites, Peter Johnston, Martin Kratz
        p.   cm.
    Bibliography: p.
    Includes index.
    ISBN: 0-442-28532-9 (pbk.)
    1. Computer viruses. I. Johnston, Peter, 1948- . II. Kratz, Martin P. J. III.
    Title
    QA76.76.C68F57 1989
    005.8--dc19   88-13496

CONTENTS

PREFACE

Do you worry about computer virus programs? If you use personal computers, and especially if you frequently use bulletin boards, perhaps you should. This book provides accurate information to help you learn what the whole virus phenomenon is about. You'll find checklists to help you cope with a virus problem, and lists of symptoms to help you diagnose your problem as a virus. We've provided practical tips to help you avoid virus programs in the first place. In the Appendix, there are brief reviews, with contact addresses, of antiviral products. If you're a professional, you'll find references to help you dig into technical details.

There's a party game called telephone or grapevine. People sit in a circle, one person whispers a message into the next person's ear, that person whispers the message into the next person's ear, and so on around the circle. The last listener then compares what was heard to what was whispered by the first person in the chain. Normally, the message is totally garbled by the time it gets back around the circle to the first person.

Some of the general press reports about computer virus programs in the past few months remind us of this party game. The first report, say in the *Wall Street Journal*, is reasonably detailed. (To a security professional, it shows evidence of a reporter who doesn't really understand the situation but takes good notes and writes well.) The story goes out over the wire services; it's edited to fit other newspapers' needs (often by people who have no technical knowledge at all), and by the time a local paper prints it, there's almost no resemblance to the original story.

The authors of this book all practice in areas that lead to advising clients on computer security or legal matters. During lunch one day, two of us were lamenting the garbled press reports and debating how we could serve our clients better by being ready to help them cope with computer virus programs. We knew of the *MacMag* virus on the Macintosh that startled users on March 2, 1988. Viruses had not been much of a problem in the past but with the sudden publicity we expected (and still expect) them to become a very big problem.

At some point in that discussion, one of us said, "Why don't we write a book." The book you are reading is the result.

We've compiled the available information into one book and written it using language understandable to people without in-depth technical backgrounds. By knowing the technical issues, we've avoided the inaccuracies sometimes found in articles written by people who don't really understand the technical issues but simply take notes.

The Computer Virus Crisis will help people who are, or think they are, or may soon be, coping with a computer virus. Although the level is relatively non-technical, we have included sufficient technical detail to help those who have some background to understand what some of the exposures are, how to recognize when they have a virus, and what to do about it if they do. If you need more information, refer to the Appendix, which is a review of some antiviral products. Some packages include detailed technical hints, along with instructions on how to use the tools provided. We recommend that you check out the vaccines and other protection software.

In *Through the Looking Glass and What Alice Found There*, Lewis Carroll has a character say, "When I use a word, it means just what I choose it to mean--neither more nor less." Since there's considerable confusion (even among professionals) about many words used in the area of computer security, we've included a Glossary. Use the definitions to help you in this book as well as others. It's ever so much more fruitful to talk about things when everyone's using the same words to mean the same things.

This book is not the last word on computer virus programs. Many vandals are working very hard to create viruses and many professionals are working to devise protection methods and products. Things change extremely quickly, far more quickly than a book can reflect. With this book as a base, you'll know enough about what the situation is to be able to follow the current material from magazines and journals.

In many places in this book, we present illustrative material designed to explain how a computer virus can do what it does. When we were creating these examples, we had a dilemma: If we made the examples absolutely complete and functional, we would in effect provide a "cookbook" that could very easily be used by vandals to produce a virus. That is not our desire or purpose. We do not want to promote the spread of viruses. The examples are therefore detailed and complete enough to illustrate the points, but not enough to produce a virus. What we want to do is help average computer users understand what computer virus programs are about and how to guard against them. When you understand what is going on, your use of computers will be safer.

The professionals and programmers who read this will easily identify the missing information *because they already have this background knowledge*--it is part of the working tools of our profession.

In creating this book, we have had considerable support from many people. Some of the software developers whose products are reviewed in the Appendix provided not only copies of their products for review, but also information their own research staffs have accumulated. Mr. Ian Fraser, owner of Microcomputer And Graphic Image Consultants Inc., helped out with much of the technical detail in Chapter 5 and reviews of the DOS antiviral programs in the Appendix. Dr. H. Highland, editor-in-chief of *Computers and Security*, is working at a very technical level and helped us with numerous references and some reports of what his team is discovering. Dianne Littwin and Maud Keisman of Van Nostrand Reinhold have worked closely with us to accomplish publishing a quality book as quickly as possible. Ms. Harriet Serenkin offered invaluable advice in revising drafts.

We first heard the phrase "safe hex" from Michael Cervansky, Vice President of Sophco in Boulder Colorado. We found that the phrase is highly recognizable to lay as well as professional computer users and chose to use it to give people a memorable description of the group of protective measures that minimize your chances of problems with virus programs.

Except for one poster reproduction, the book was created entirely using computer tools. Drafts were printed on a laser printer at Galbraith Law Offices, and the typesetting was done from the same PostScript files by the University of Alberta Printing Services.

After reading this book, we hope you will see that viruses are not all that magical or mythical. They unfortunately can be produced and spread by all too many individuals. We hope this book will make you more aware of the problem. Once you are aware, your chance of being exposed or, if exposed, infected, is less. We want you to practice safe hex.

As a final point, we want you to know that we consider introducing viruses into other people's computer systems unethical, unprofessional, and unlawful. *Don't do it!*

Chapter 1

INTRODUCTION

Is today the day? I know there's something important I must do if the time is right. No, it's not Friday the 13th yet. Let's see now: If today isn't the day, I have to reproduce myself. Let's look at the system files; I know there will be one, every computer has one. There's one: Is there one of me there already? If there isn't, I can copy myself. No, I'm already in that program; let's check out this computer's program files. Surely there's at least one where I haven't been yet. Yes, there's one, and I found it after only 48 tries. Oh, it's marked read-only; that's OK, I'll just change that marking so I can change the file. This feels good; I'm copying myself into that program; now I change the program just a bit, a little jump here and a return there, after my copy. I remember changing something--oh, yes, change the file back to read-only. Now, did I cover my tracks? Let's see, all the attributes are the same as when I got here; the length hasn't changed since I found some empty space to copy myself into. I must remember to change the creation date back to what it was when I got here, too. No point in making it easy to see where I've been. Am I finished yet? No; I need to go through the same process on the diskette drives, if there are any, and see if I can reach through a network too. Am I finished now? Yes--oh, that's what I'm supposed to do on Friday 13th! I wonder what FORMAT C: means? Hey, I'm supposed to do that if I've made fifty copies of myself. And I was already at forty-nine. Next time . . . .

You've just been introduced to what a computer virus might be thinking (if it could think) as it goes about its business. There have been viruses that worked exactly that way. You wouldn't even know the virus was in your system, until something went wrong. Then you not only have to fix the visible damage, but you also have to find any place the virus might have made copies of itself.

You can be very safe, of course. You could purchase a machine from a trusted manufacturer, write all of your own programs, never use anyone else's programs, and never communicate with another computer. As long as your trusted manufacturer is really careful, you would not be risking exposure to viruses. You also would not have a very useful computer, and you wouldn't be taking part in one of the things that is changing our world in ways never before possible in human history.

There are other ways you can protect yourself; some even offer good protection. The purpose of this book is to tell you the real story about computer virus programs, and help you protect yourself against them without missing out on the information revolution.

USING THIS BOOK

This book contains four kinds of information: moderately technical information; references for other reading on security in general and viruses in particular; reviews of antiviral products in the Appendix and definitions in the Glossary; and general information about the whole computer virus phenomenon.

If you think you've got a computer virus, turn to the Appendix *immediately*, and contact one of the vaccine developers to begin solving your problem. While you're waiting for your new vaccine, look at Chapters 8 and 9; they contain several hints about what to do. After you've cleaned up everything, look at Chapters 4 and 7, for suggestions on how to avoid future problems.

If you just want to learn about viruses, continue reading. If you already know a fair bit, look at Chapter 5, which has the most technical material.

If you're thinking that it might be good fun to create and spread a virus, read Chapters 10 and 11, where you'll see that it's against the law. Then read Chapter 6, which describes some of the bad effects that unethical people who spread computer diseases cause for everyone else. *Don't do it!* You make things worse for yourself as well as for the rest of us.

How Viruses Affect You

In the past few months, the press has published many reports about computer viruses. There's been a real outbreak, with the impetus probably provided by the triggering of the *MacMag* "Peace" virus in March 1988.[1] Unfortunately, some of the material has been sensational or garbled, such as a report that every computer in Seattle has a virus. In reality, computer viruses don't spread like the

---

[1] See [Peace Virus 1988], [O'Connor 1988]. This virus was first reported around February 1988. It's referred to either as the *MacMag* virus or as the peace virus. We believe in assigning responsibility where due, and use the perpetrators' name.

common cold. They aren't intelligent; they don't hate you; and it's not even very difficult to avoid most exposures.

But there have been, and there are now, some pretty nasty viruses floating around in computers. Some developments in the past few years have increased people's exposure. If you communicate with other computers, especially if you download programs from public bulletin boards, your risk could be high. If you accept pirate copies of software from people you don't know (or even if you do know the source of your copy, but not the source of the other person's copy), your risk could be *very* high.

On the other hand, if you have programs that you purchased in shrink wrap and perhaps an electronic mail setup, your risk isn't too great.

You need to ask yourself, "Does anyone dislike *me* that much?" If you're a specific target, you need to take precautions. If you're just John User (or Jane User) you'll probably never have a problem if you simply apply some common sense.

WHAT'S THE PROBLEM?

About 10 years ago, one of us needed to run a job as cheaply as possible on a time-sharing system. The job would take a while to run and had to wait for other higher priority, and higher-paying, jobs. It was late Friday afternoon. A small file was created that would check to see if the job had run; if it had run, commands in the file would direct output appropriately and clean things up; if it had not run, it would submit itself into the job queue again. In this way, the job would be sure to get the lowest rate, and the author could go home rather than wait around Friday evening.

Unfortunately, the command file wasn't tested carefully enough. It wound up submitting itself repeatedly. In fact, as soon as the job actually did run, the command file went wild. Ten minutes after the system was started up on Sunday, the author got a polite and rather pointed call from the system administrator, who wanted the 4096 copies of the same job deleted from the job queue so someone else could get in (Figure 1.1). The situation wasn't intentional, but its effect was to create a quasi-virus and put it into a system. (It was fixed, with much embarrassment, taking about 15 minutes and several utilities to get rid of all those jobs.)

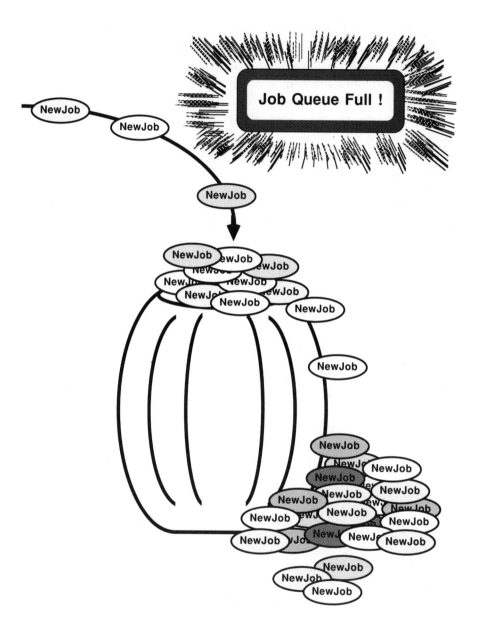

Figure 1.1 Too Many Jobs

Fred Cohen hadn't coined the term "virus" yet,[2] but that command file fit his later description. The point of the story is that a virus isn't anything new, magical, or otherwise unknown, in spite of what you can read today.

But if the concept of a virus isn't really new, and it's not very difficult to create one, even accidentally, why is there suddenly a problem? Partly, it's because the increasing compatibility of computers and communications have made it possible for a virus to spread much farther, faster, and easier than was possible in the past. And partly, it's because a lot more people, in fact millions, now use computers. (See Chapter 2 for the "connectivity" issue.)

Take a look at the kind of people who could create a virus. They have to have some skill with computers, especially writing programs. They have to have some kind of access to a computer, specifically to yours. They have to have a reason to spread a virus. Most likely, millions of people have the skills to create a virus, on purpose or accidentally. Any computer science student and a whole lot of bright youngsters with computers have the skills.

Professionals can, of course, create virus programs. But they think of the return from their effort. Before they do something, they ask, "Is there an easier and safer way to achieve my objective?" There have not been many computer viruses spread by professionals for the simple reason that those who want to destroy or damage programs or computers have easier ways to do it.

There *are* people with professional skills and training who desire to mess up computer systems. Terrorists and spies, as well as legitimate professionals, possess the needed skills. To date, they've had better results by doing things like attacking power supplies and bribing bank tellers. It's probable that the current rash of viruses wasn't created and spread by professionals to achieve an objective.

There's another category of people. We call them vandals. Their motivation is to throw a monkey wrench into the works and watch the sparks fly or to demonstrate how superior their minds are (as judged by themselves) by cracking computer systems. They're not usually looking for gain, and they don't care that the return may be less than the risk and cost. They are the kind of people who slash paintings in museums, throw rocks through windows, and generally are rather nasty and pitiful examples of human being. If people like this have technical skills, they might create a computer virus.

---

[2][Cohen 1984].

WHAT IS A COMPUTER VIRUS?

A computer virus can be defined as malicious software which replicates itself.[3] This definition is a little biased for our purposes: A virus need not be malicious. The key things about a computer virus are that it reproduces itself, and can reproduce itself in systems other than the one in which it was created; and that it can somehow attach itself to other programs (see the Glossary and Chapter 2). The command file example mentioned earlier is almost a virus: It reproduced and denied access to that system (malicious, although not intended that way), and it would have done the same on any of the other computer systems maintained by that company if it had been copied; it didn't infect any other programs, however.

A virus is just a name for a class of programs. They reproduce and infect other programs. Beyond that they could do anything any other program can (see Chapter 3 for more).

You may run into another sort of computer vermin, the *worm*. It is a program that "worms" its way through a system, altering small bits of data or code whenever it can get access (Figure 1.2).

A virus might also be a worm; if a worm *reproduces* itself in other systems and *infects* other programs, it would also be a virus.

Note that a computer virus is a program and it has to be *run* in order to reproduce or to do any damage. This fact is the key to several of the protection strategies discussed later.

HOW DOES A VIRUS SPREAD?

A computer virus does *not* spread through the air. You can't get it by shaking hands, or touching a doorknob, or by having someone next to you sneeze. A computer virus must be *put* into your computer by you or by someone else. One way a computer virus can be put into your system is as a *Trojan Horse*. A Trojan Horse (see Chapter 2 and Figure 1.4) is, for our purposes, a program that seems to do one thing but also does something else.

---

[3]See [Podell 1987] for a similar definition.

ABCD	IJKL	QRST	ABCD	IJKL	QRST
0000	0000	UVWX	EFGH	MNOP	UVWX
IJKL	0000	ABCD	0000	0000	ABCD
0000	0000	EFGH	0000	0000	0000
0000	0000	0000	0000	0000	0000
UVWX	EFGH	MNOP	UVWX	0000	MNOP
ABCD	IJKL	QRST	ABCD	0000	QRST
EFGH	MNOP	UVWX	EFGH	0000	0000

Figure 1.2 Worm Tracks

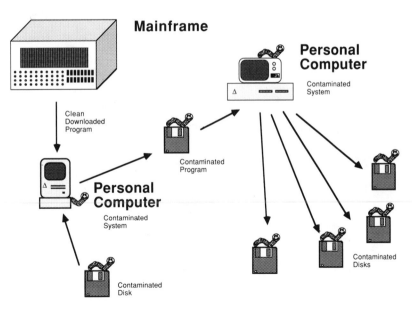

Figure 1.3 How a Virus Spreads

Figure 1.4 Trojan Horse

Worldwide Communications in the 1980s

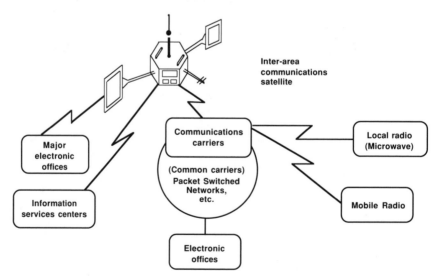

Figure 1.5 Worldwide Communications

We've said that computer viruses don't spread through the air and must be put into your system. This leaves an enormous number of possible infection pathways. For example, any time you download a program from another computer, or run a program from a diskette you've obtained, whether purchased, swapped, or borrowed, there is some exposure. Moreover, someone can tap telephone lines and insert a virus into your system--but this is not an easy task: Is there someone who dislikes *you personally* that much?

If you run a widely known bulletin board system (BBS), however, you might want to think about this. If you're an oil company transmitting exploration data, you're known to be at risk of corporate spying although probably not to viruses. If you're a government, you'd better plan on the enemy trying to put viruses into the computers that run your telephone system and your military communications in the event of war. If you are an individual microcomputer user, your exposure probably is not nearly as great.[4]

Different activities expose you to different risks. You can minimize your risk by practicing safe hex; simple common-sense measures that will cut your exposure to a very low level (see Chapter 7). These include things like avoiding pirate software, checking programs you download from a BBS before you run them, and using one or more of the antivirus tools described in the Appendix. Make sure you have good backups of your files and programs so you can recover from damage done by a virus (or by a power failure or static discharge, which is much more common).

Spreading Viruses Through Connectivity

The real reason computer viruses are becoming a serious problem, and could be catastrophic in the future, is linked to one of the long-term trends in the development of computers: connectivity. This issue is looked at in more detail in Chapter 2. For now, think of connectivity as something that makes it possible for you to use your microcomputer to contact other computers, anywhere in the world, even if the other machines don't have the same operating system (see Figure 1.5).

One of the things connectivity means is that other people can run programs you wrote, and you can run programs they wrote. If they decide to spread a virus, connectivity means it may infect you, or vice versa

Connectivity also opens up some extra points of attack for people trying to put a virus into your system. Since communications is necessary for connectivity,

---

[4]It's much greater than being hit by lightning, though. There were 400 injuries or deaths from lightning in the US in 1987, or about 1 in 500,000. 350,000 Mac users were hit by the *MacMag* virus in 1988, about 1 in 5.

people can attack the communications networks as well as trying to reach you through infected diskettes.

Today, connectivity is a growing concept. So far, different operating systems aren't very compatible, and a virus that infects DOS microcomputers won't bother a Macintosh computer or a mainframe. But this will change soon. Connectivity implies eventually that the same virus can infect mainframes and minicomputers, as well as microcomputers.

Viruses and IBM and Compatible Microcomputers

There are estimates that over 10 million microcomputers using the PC-DOS or MS-DOS operating system (IBM compatible computers) have been sold. One of the wonderful things about this is that since the microcomputers all use the same (or nearly the same) operating system, programs written for one computer will work on most others. This means that you can buy a complex word processor or spreadsheet, and the development costs are shared among hundreds or thousands of people so the cost to each individual or company is relatively small.

This is a blessing and a curse: Without conventions, you could not have the same software on millions of machines; with conventions, everyone knows where to put a virus, and anyone who finds a vulnerable spot knows it applies essentially everywhere.

Macintosh World

The Macintosh world is also one of shared conventions, only more so. The developers of Macintosh (Apple Computers, Inc.) have made sure that all Macintosh programs have a standard user interface. This means that you can run most any program on any Mac without needing to learn new command languages. The standard interface makes it easy to work with Macs; you don't need to be concerned with what happens at the system level; in fact, you are shielded from such things. But it also means that unless you use special tools, you can't even *see* the effects of a virus. It's easier to hide a virus on a Mac than on an IBM or compatible machine.

Other Microcomputer Operating Systems

To prevent this book from becoming too technical, and the discussion too fragmented, we only use the MS/PC-DOS and Macintosh operating systems for our examples. Other microcomputer operating systems are vulnerable and have been reported to have viruses, as well. There are reports of virus programs loose in Commodore Amiga machines, and in the Apple II series.

Spreading Viruses Through Networks: WAN and LAN

Computers can be linked together in networks. LANs--Local Area Networks--and WANs--Wide Area Networks[5]--describe groups of systems that can communicate with each other (Figure 1.6). With the proper networks, even computers with different operating systems, like Macs and DOS machines, can transfer data and (sometimes) programs.

Wide Area Network (WAN)

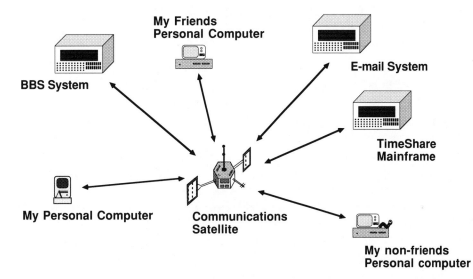

Figure 1.6 Wide Area Networks (WAN)

Because of this linkage, a network has to be more careful about computer viruses. You may be exposed to a virus even though you personally practice safe hex, just because someone managed to put a virus into the network somewhere, perhaps on the other side of the world in the case of a WAN.

---

[5]For complete definitions see the Glossary and Chapter 2.

Viruses and Minicomputers

There haven't been too many reports of viruses on minicomputers. It's not clear why; there's no inherent reason why a virus won't work on a mini. Perhaps the exposure is less because most minicomputers are intended to support many users at the same time and their operating systems have better security built in. (DOS and other microcomputer operating systems were designed for a single user and originally had *no* security built in.)

Operating systems like UNIX variants and VAX/VMS are found on many minicomputers; UNIX variants are available on microcomputers and soon may become common. It seems likely that before long minicomputers will use the same software and operating system (UNIX) as some microcomputers and thus minicomputers will be exposed to pretty much the same viruses.

Viruses and Mainframes

Mainframe computers are less vulnerable to viruses than microcomputers for two reasons: First, their operating systems are very complex and have built-in security; second, each implementation of a mainframe is pretty much unique, and most viruses that attack one mainframe won't attack another successfully. Even the same operating system, implemented on two different mainframe configurations, may not be very vulnerable to a virus from a different system.[6]

Another reason for lower vulnerability to viruses on mainframe systems is that any mainframe environment includes professionals who know what computer viruses are. When the system "acts funny," a professional is trained to *stop and find out what's going on*. A virus tends to be noticed very quickly in such an environment whereas it might go unnoticed for a long time in some microcomputer environments.

Mainframe systems often support thousands of users. Therefore, although a virus that attacks one mainframe may not be very dangerous to another, it's dangerous to everyone using that first mainframe computer. University and research computing environments have been notoriously vulnerable to viruses and other program problems.[7] They have many users, of many different classifications. Some are students, who traditionally "play jokes" on one another and

---

[6]Although a FORTRAN or COBOL program may run on several mainframe systems, it's nearly always necessary to recompile it, and usually necessary to make other modifications as well. At the level at which viruses work, different mainframes really don't share many vulnerabilities. Note that this poses no problem to using a mainframe as a *medium* to transmit viruses from one microcomputer to another; then it doesn't matter what the mainframe is like, since the virus is part of a file that looks like any other data file to the mainframe.

[7]See the CRABS, BRAIN, PLO viruses described in Chapter 2.

have perpetrated some fairly serious computer sabotage;[8] and some are engaged in research that may involve poorly understood concepts (which can have side effects). Also, generally security has not been a real concern at university computing centers.

Viruses and Distributed Systems

A distributed (or dispersed) system is like a network (WAN or LAN), only more so. The user may not even be aware of the location of the programs and data files being used. In fact, the location may change from time to time as areas of the dispersed system are freed up and new things move into them. In that environment, it's even less likely than in a LAN or WAN environment that an individual can control exposure to a virus. The exposure of the distributed system has to be controlled at a system-wide level, and the individual user can only trust the system administrators.

Spreading Viruses Through Software Piracy

We'll discuss piracy in Chapter 6. For now, consider that copying programs without paying for them is theft.[9] If you accept pirate software from someone, you are accepting stolen goods. How sure can you be that the lack of morality doesn't extend to including a virus before passing along the illegitimate copy?

What to Do about Viruses?

First, be aware of how your computer works. A change in appearance of an icon on a Macintosh, for example, may be a warning that a virus is around. Unexpected actions, especially disk read/write operations when you didn't ask the program to save anything, are warning signs. If the amount of RAM (memory) available suddenly decreases, find out why. (In DOS, if you use a shell program like *Windows*, or any of several memory resident aids, it's trivial to check available RAM. On the Macintosh, select "About the Finder . . . " or use one of several commercial or shareware Desk Accessories or applications.) You may have a memory resident virus (see TSR in the Glossary and Chapters 2 and 5) or you might just have a print spooler loaded.

---

[8]For instance, there was a landmark case in Canada involving "theft of telecommunications," where two students seriously damaged a number of corporate data bases on the local university's computer.

[9]It may or may not be defined as theft in law, depending on where you live; but it is at least copyright violation. It deprives the software author of a fair return for the significant investment in developing the software package.

All of these symptoms just as well might be caused by bugs (that is, errors) in your software. Software bugs are a lot more likely than viruses, unless you download and run every new program as soon as it appears on a BBS. Chapter 8 presents a closer look at diagnosis.

Avoiding Viruses

The list is just a teaser; Chapter 7 has the details.

1. Practice safe hex: Never accept pirate copies of software; use only programs that come in their original shrink-wrapped package; always test a program before you run it; use one or more of the vaccine-type programs listed in the Appendix to search for known viruses; before you run a program, open it as a data file with your word processor (in read-only mode if you have that capability), and look for readable messages in the garbage;[10] don't run the program if you find something like "HA HA GOTCHA;" be *very* careful about anything you get from a public-domain bulletin board, especially games.

2. *Keep backups.* Then if your program does get infected, you can replace it with the original uninfected copy.[11] Use write-protect tabs on the backup diskettes for added protection.

3. Be realistic; you probably don't have to worry too much. Most computer viruses can be avoided simply by using some common sense.

There are ways to accomplish what you need to and still be reasonably safe from virus infection. Chapter 7 goes into things you can do, or not do, which will help you to avoid letting a computer virus into your system.

Getting Rid of Viruses

(Chapter 9 has the details on how to get rid of a computer virus.)

Once you have a virus, you have to get rid of it. By the time you discover the virus, it probably has copied itself many times into many programs. You need a way to track down all the copies and destroy them. The easy way is to have an *ORIGINAL WRITE-PROTECTED* backup copy of your operating system on a

---

[10]Normally, you won't be able to read anything except text messages, and those only if they're not compressed or encoded somehow. These should be things like menu displays, error messages, and copyright notices. Opening a program as a file in a word processor has dangers, by the way. *Don't change anything!* And *don't save the file.*

[11]We're going to be repetitive about backups in this book. It's so important to keep them, we think it's worth saying it again and again. This one action, if practiced regularly, will more than repay you the price of this book.

diskette; boot your system from that original system diskette (be sure it's write-protected to minimize the chance of the virus infecting your backup disk), format your hard disk, and start over from backups. That system works if you have clean backups, but it's a pretty drastic measure and takes a lot of your time. Many of the antiviral programs noted in the Appendix have capabilities that allow you to rid yourself of an infection in a somewhat less dramatic fashion. They work to varying degrees, so read the description, our comments, and the package instructions carefully.

Let's define a new word here: FUBAR, which stands for *Fouled Up Beyond All Recognition*. It's probably not new to anyone who writes programs. It describes a situation in which you know something is wrong, but everything is so messed up that you can't even be sure what's wrong, much less have any idea how to fix it. All good programs have a FUBAR routine to trap problems that weren't anticipated by the designer without blowing up messily in the face of the user. If you find yourself in the position of having to fix the damage done by a virus, your favorite file-fixing tool can't do the job, and you don't have reasonably current backups of your files, you will get a personal appreciation of what FUBAR means.

Fixing the Damage

Depending on your strategy for getting rid of a virus, you may try to repair the damage yourself. Some of the programs noted in the Appendix can search programs for viruses and kill the ones they find. If the virus has merely altered things in your File Allocation Tables (FAT), you may be able to recreate your files using special tools, called utilities. Common examples are *Norton Utilities* and *PCTOOLS* for DOS systems and *Disk 1st Aid*, *MacTools*, and *ResEdit* for the Macintosh. *If you know what you're doing*, these tools will allow you to fix just about anything repairable that a virus can do. But tools like this are dangerous. If you don't know what you're doing, you can do more damage by accident than most computer viruses do on purpose. We talk about these things in Chapter 9.

Not all damage can be fixed. A psychotic or diseased program can actually cause physical damage to parts of your computer, which can't be fixed by any program. If your data are messed up enough, it may not be possible to fix the files, or at best it may take longer than reentering the data. Your *only* protection then is your backups. You *did* make backups, didn't you?

WHAT SOFTWARE PUBLISHERS CAN DO

Very simply, software publishers can minimize any chance that a virus will be spread along with their programs by:

- Being certain their own shops are "sterile;"
- Ensuring that all steps involved in manufacturing and assembly are sterile;
- Encoding programs or capturing signatures; and
- Sending the correct signature, or key, by a different method than the program disks themselves. One way is to send out the key or signature when the purchaser returns a registration card.

If the programs are clean to start with, and if they haven't changed before they get to the purchaser (as verified by a correct signature), at least the developer won't be spreading diseased software. It's likely that there is a legal obligation for the developer to be sure that programs are free of disease when shrink-wrapped. We'll discuss the topic of what developers can do in Chapter 12, and consider legal liability in Chapter 10.

Chapter 2

DIMENSIONS OF COMPUTER VIRUSES

I remember the good old days, when computers were mainframes, analysts were magicians, and programmers punched cards.

The history of computer virus programs is a small part of the history of people's attempts to do undesirable things with computers. This chapter describes some of the methods--today we'd call them subversive programs--that have been used to mess up computers for so long that many of them even have names, like logic bomb and Salami technique. Many programmers can tell tales of the pranks programmers play on each other. Our own experience with this sort of thing goes back to the mid 1960s; to be honest, we regarded the whole thing as an intellectual challenge and good training as we competed with one another to come up with better practical jokes. In those days, "hacker" did not have any nasty connotations.

Things have changed a lot since then. There were relatively few people using computers then; now there are millions. There were only a few computers around; today there are again millions. Unfortunately, any group of people contains a percentage of undesirables; the group of computer users is now large enough to contain more than a few crooks and vandals.

Computer virus programs as a specific thing are pretty new, at least in the published literature. The first publication of the concept was in a paper at a security conference in 1984.[1] Fred Cohen developed this rather disturbing concept in 1983 when he was a graduate student, and presented it to the conference. Others picked up on the idea; *Scientific American* covered similar topics in some of the "Computer Recreations" columns in 1984, 1985, and 1987.[2] Today, with the exposure of a lot of people, there is great interest on many fronts.

---

[1] See [Cohen 1984].

[2] See Dewdney [1984, 1985 #1, 1985 # 2, 1987].

Earlier, we described how one of us unintentionally created a near-virus in 1978. Although we haven't seen any earlier published reports, we suspect that unintentional or intentional virus programs existed even before 1978. The concepts involved aren't very difficult. Over the years viruses have progressed from being an interesting potential nuisance to a very real problem. The biggest reason for graduating from minor annoyance to serious risk is the linking together of millions of computers using the same operating systems and application programs, plus almost universal connectivity among computers by telephone.

COMMUNICATION, CONNECTIVITY, AND THE SPREAD OF VIRUSES

Computer virus programs can be a real nuisance if your co-worker or best friend gives you one as a joke. Still, that doesn't make them very drastic, and unless there's a mistake no real damage is done. But what about a stranger? Or what about a stranger in another country? If you're in Italy, how about a Red Brigade virus? If you're in England, how about an Irish Republican Army virus? How about your ex-spouse, the one who's suing you for custody now? How about your ex-employee, the one you fired last week?

Suddenly, the notion of a virus gets more serious. For one thing, we're outside the bounds of common sense that put limits on what your co-worker or friend is likely to do. For another, in the above scenarios, the person who might send you a virus is out to do you serious damage. And for yet another, he or she could be anywhere on the planet, as long as there's a telephone connection.

Something is happening to our planet at an increasing rate. Two hundred years ago, most people died within 30 miles of their birthplace. Sixty years ago, a trip from one coast in North America to another took a week or more. Today one of us talked from home to people in New York, Maryland, Toronto, Washington, and Pheonix. Another communicated via electronic mail with computer systems in New York, Florida, and California. We can sign on with our computers to a network that has hundreds of thousands of users all over North America and send e-mail that will reach anyone else on the network in minutes, wherever they are on Earth. That's one of the things that's happening to computers: communications (Figure 2.1).

Worldwide Communications Networks

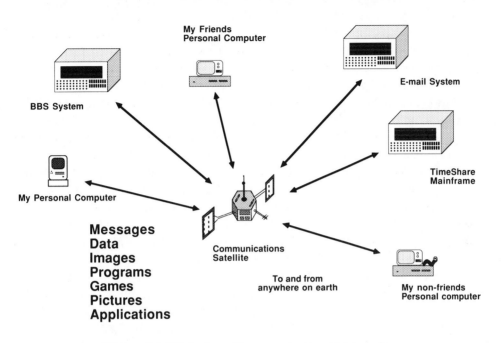

Figure 2.1 Wide Area Communications Networks

IBM Christmas Card and *MacMag* Virus

Let's take a look at two examples that illustrate viruses and communications: the IBM Christmas card and the *MacMag* virus. Both began to spread about the same time, in December 1987. One was a virus, and it's not certain what the other was.

In the Christmas card incident, a program began life in EARN, the European academic network. It's reported to have spread as an electronic mail message. The program seemed to draw a Christmas card on a screen--but in the background it was also reading the files containing addresses of incoming and outgoing mail and sending copies of itself to all available addresses. Pretty quickly, the Christmas card got into Bitnet (a North American academic system that includes electronic mail capabilities). Shortly, IBM's worldwide PROFS electronic mail system was clogged up with copies of the Christmas card.[3] The mail system stayed clogged for some time, until technicians could isolate parts of the system and remove all copies of the Christmas card program.

In this example, something that originated in Germany spread over most of the non-communist world in a very short time. Even if it wasn't a virus, it affected thousands of people by clogging up the mail system with copies of itself. Here, a mainframe-based electronic mail network was the target.

Our second example is similar, only this time it's microcomputers, specifically Macintosh microcomputers, we're looking at. As reported in several media in April and May 1988, in December 1987 the Montreal publisher of *MacMag* magazine left a "benign" virus on two machines in a computer store in the same building as the magazine's offices. The reports say that on March 2, 1988 the virus was triggered and an estimated 350,000 machines worldwide displayed a "Peace" message when the computers were started up. The virus then erased itself from the system and everything proceeded normally.

This virus spread by several means. The really frightening way was by commercial shrink-wrapped software: Somehow, the virus infected something in Aldus Corporation's operation before the software program *Freehand* was packaged, and diseased copies were distributed unknowingly. This has sent a shiver through a lot of software producers and purchasers: Even shrink-wrapped software may not be safe.[4] What if that virus had *not* been benign?[5]

We've actually looked at something a lot more important than simple communications in these two examples. The thing that makes the viruses so frightening is the sheer *number* of computers and people affected. The electronic mail Christmas card filled up the mail space on several kinds of computers, all linked in some fashion into EARN or Bitnet. The Macintosh *MacMag* virus affected hundreds of thousands of machines. It's no longer true that computers are reasonably safe from each other.

---

[3]The Christmas card may not a virus by our definition, but rather a form of worm. The program did not attach itself to any other program; it only sent copies of itself through a mail system. There are conflicting reports about this incident as well; when we contacted IBM in January they would only confirm that the mail system did get clogged up. The spread appears to have taken a day or so; the cleanup may have taken about three days.

[4]By the time this book is in your hands, we expect software producers to have taken steps to make sure this kind of thing doesn't happen again. Aldus quite responsibly publicized the infection and offered various kinds of assistance to users who may have purchased diseased packages.

[5]If you're a science fiction fan, check out Richmond, *Challenge the Hellmaker*, and E. E. Smith, Family d'Alembert #10 *Revolt of the Galaxy*. Both describe connectivity and communications that allow people (or in one case an intelligent computer) in one place to affect computers in many other places. One of the instances is fairly benign; one is not nice at all. Both are pretty disruptive if you're the owner of the computer involved.

This shared vulnerability means that people almost can forget what computer their material is on and where the computer is--but it also means that we're all susceptible to attack.

How Fast a Virus Can Spread

As modem prices continue to tumble and more and more systems communicate, the rate and distance over which a virus can spread becomes scarcely believable. Consider what happened when one of us downloaded, through a combination of packet-switched networks and on-line bulletin boards, a program that was placed into the public domain in Europe less than three hours earlier. During that time the program had migrated through three Bulletin Board Systems.

Now look at Figure 2.2 for some numbers illustrating exponential growth. We developed Figure 2.2 on the basis of each person distributing information (a secret, a program, a joke, or whatever) to just four other people within three hours (the same numbers as in the program download example). During the next three hours, each of the four people passes the material on to another four, and so on. Within two days, the information has spread to more people than exist in the world today.

Admittedly this is a contrived example; sooner or later someone in the chain will pass the information back to someone who has already heard it (remember how suddenly you seem to hear the same new joke from everyone you meet, even in different cities?); some people will not pass it on; some will pass it on but after distorting it to uselessness. With the ease of contacting electronic mail and BBSs, and with the growing interconnections among these systems, we have to consider just how fast information or a virus can spread.

There are enormous benefits from having greater and greater linkage and being able to run the same programs anywhere. In fact, there's a clear trend to have computers, whether mainframes or microcomputers, able to run the same programs and operating systems and to connect various systems.[6] We call this trend to link up computers with common file formats and programs *connectivity*.

Connectivity means people can share data, programs, and computers. Unfortunately, it also means that vandals can attack everyone with the same computer virus programs.[7]

---

[6]Digital with their VAX strategies, IBM's SAA, and efforts with UNIX by several groups are examples.

[7]See [Madsen 1988] for a (somewhat technical) description of some exposures resulting from this kind of connectivity.

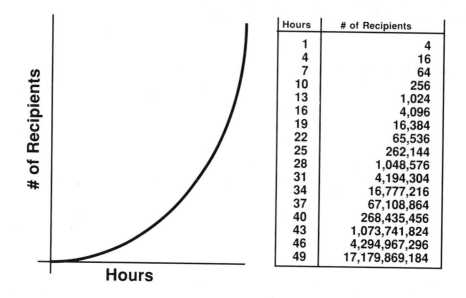

Hours	# of Recipients
1	4
4	16
7	64
10	256
13	1,024
16	4,096
19	16,384
22	65,536
25	262,144
28	1,048,576
31	4,194,304
34	16,777,216
37	67,108,864
40	268,435,456
43	1,073,741,824
46	4,294,967,296
49	17,179,869,184

Figure 2.2 Exponential Growth

WHY DO WE CALL IT A VIRUS?

In medicine (from a layman's perspective), a virus is a kind of disease-spreading thing that is very small and hard to find, which enters cells and attaches itself to them so that when the cell multiplies so does the virus. Under some circumstances it can explode into action, which may even destroy the infected organism. In people, viruses are thought to cause varieties of the common cold, smallpox, polio, and HIV which is linked with AIDS.[8] Some viruses spread very easily (such as smallpox or the common cold); some don't spread as easily (such as AIDS).

---

[8]AIDS is Acquired Immune Deficiency Syndrome. The virus is spread by sexual contact or exchange of bodily fluids such as contaminated blood.

Computer viruses are computer programs, just like any other program. People who create them have given these programs the ability to attach themselves to other programs, to make copies of themselves, and under some circumstances to damage computer systems, data, or programs stored in them. The name "virus" is used because many of the characteristics of these programs mimic the characteristics of disease viruses.

Hiding and Replicating Itself

Computer virus programs are designed to attach themselves to other programs. Additionally, many of them are designed to use very sophisticated methods of hiding themselves from you, the victim. The qualities of attaching themselves to other programs and hiding their presence place viruses in the class of "hidden code" penetration methods; the general term for this class of program is Trojan Horse.

In Homer's *Iliad*, the Greeks, after many unsuccessful tries to defeat Troy, finally got their soldiers inside Troy's walls by using a ruse now called a Trojan Horse. The Trojans worshipped a god in the form of a horse. The Greeks constructed an idol of such a horse and left it for the Trojans to take while the Greeks apparently withdrew, leaving victory to Troy. The horse, however, was hollowed, and contained Greek soldiers. When the Trojans took the idol inside the city, the Greek soldiers were able to open the gates and let the Greek army inside the city, and Troy fell.

Computer virus programs use a similar strategy to spread: They attach themselves to other programs that do neat things, and get into your system when you run the useful or interesting program. Then the virus copies itself into every place it can reach--replicating--and may sit and wait for some signal.

Spreading

Usually, the first thing a virus program does is make copies of itself. It will try to attach itself to a place in your system where it can get itself run along with something useful. Because of the speeds at which computers work, a virus can make a *lot* of copies of itself in seconds. If it can get into a network or Bulletin Board System, it can spread to thousands or millions of users within weeks or even days. The *MacMag* virus and the IBM Christmas card are graphic examples.

So far, the virus program has attached itself to other programs, is hiding itself either passively or actively by distorting information, and is reproducing. What this does to you is use up some storage space that you probably have better uses for. This can be bad enough: The Christmas card program stopped a major international electronic mail system just by filling up all available storage capacity.

Doing Damage

The real problem happens when the virus finds whatever trigger it's waiting for and explodes into doing actual damage. Chapter 3 describes some of the things computer virus programs have been known to do. Look at Figure 2.3 for an example of one kind of damage, zeroing out some memory.

This figure shows a simulated memory in three states. In the first, there's what you want to be there. In the second, there are worm tracks: the effects of a worm program in your memory. The worm simply moves around randomly or purposefully, into any space it can reach. As it moves it copies itself into the new place and leaves behind zeros where you had useful data. It doesn't take long before those zeros mess up whatever you were doing (unless you were deliberately creating zeros). The evidence disappears when you reboot the computer: The worm might start again, depending on what program you run, or it might not. What you see is that the program you are using suddenly stops working, probably messily when it finds zeros instead of some computer instruction or control information. Since the evidence is gone after you reboot, it can be very difficult to figure out what happened.

The virus program in the bottom part of the figure goes a step further. In addition to the single copy of itself that the worm makes, the virus replicates. In this figure, each new copy of the virus starts on its own path through memory (or perhaps through your diskette); in addition to leaving worm tracks, the virus leaves copies of itself, ready to leap into action at some signal. Even if you figure out what's happening, you have to find and get rid of *all* the copies before you're safe; otherwise the whole problem starts over. Earlier, we described exponential growth. This is similar. The interval between copies may not be hours but rather tiny fractions of a second; your computer can get seriously infected in less than a second.[9]

Figure 2.3 could be your computer's memory, or the file storage on your hard disk, or some other place the virus can reach. The virus may only copy itself until it sees some signal (like Friday the 13th in the system clock); but you could have *a lot* of copies before you know you're infected.

---

[9]Experiments have indicated that a virus normally can completely infect a personal computer within two seconds of its activation.

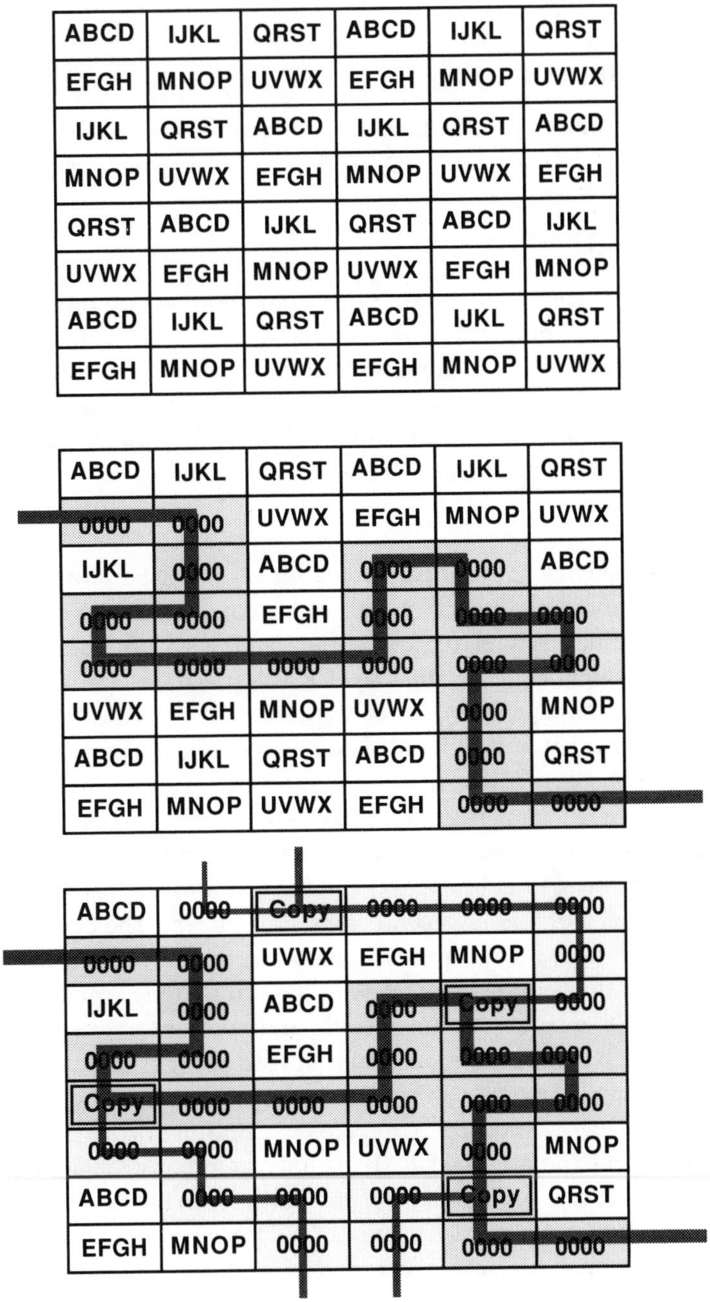

Figure 2.3 Memory, Worm Tracks, and Virus Damage

SOME FAMOUS VIRUSES

Here is a description of a few of the most famous viruses known to be out there. It should give you a feel for the kind of thing you run into with computer viruses.

Monkey-on-Your-Back

The Monkey-on-Your-Back Macintosh virus may not be around any more; people tend to get rid of programs containing a virus pretty quickly when they find out they've been infected. It is reported to have been a program that had a very attractive screen display of monkeys doing various acrobatics. While the monkeys jumped, the program made copies of itself in various places in the system, and then it trashed the hard disk file directories.

Crabs

CRABS was developed in a spirit of play at the AT&T Bell Laboratories.[10] In this research environment (and in others), it was and is common for people to "play" with the computer. Such play is fun for the participants and frequently leads to new ideas that turn out to be very valuable. CRABS was developed as part of an effort to examine the consequences of violating certain design rules of a then new kind of screen display, that now is familiar to anyone who's seen a Macintosh, a Microsoft *Windows* display, or the new *Presentation Manager*. Some other tools that are useful, such as a screen magnifying glass to enlarge part of a screen for a closer, more detailed look, were developed as part of the same research.

Figure 2.4 shows the results of CRABS running on a Macintosh screen. The top shows the screen shortly after several crabs showed up. The crabs eat away at the edges of your display, and pretty quickly the screen starts to look moth eaten. As you see in the bottom screen, it's not the sort of thing you fail to notice. You can't stop CRABS except by turning off the computer or terminal.

The original CRABS spawned clones that spread things like animal tracks across screens. It also spawned the equivalent of the vaccine programs mentioned in the Appendix, as people competed to find ways to stop CRABS, improve it, and so on. The original CRABS is not around any longer, but you'll find a version of CRABS on most university or research-oriented computer systems, and most public bulletin board systems. CRABS programs are available for DOS microcomputers, Macintosh computers, and many minicomputers or mainframes.

---

[10]CRABS is described in more technical detail by A. K. Dewdney in a *Scientific American* Computer Recreations column; see [Dewdney 1985 #2].

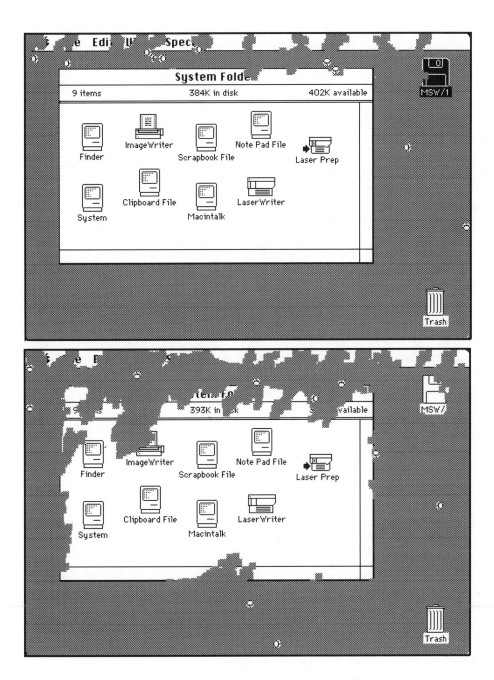

Figure 2.4 CRABS on the Macintosh

CRABS as described is a worm rather than a virus.[11] There have been reports of viruses that spread CRABS.[12]

SCORES

SCORES is another Macintosh virus. It seems to have been first reported in February 1988, although it may have existed as early as September 1987. Several symptoms have been reported, including problems using the SetStartup cdev, causing difficulties printing *Excel* and *MacDraw* files, problems running *MacDraw*, corruption of *Excel* files, and causing the running system to crash unexpectedly.

Careful investigation of infected systems has revealed two additional symptoms:

- The Scrapbook and Notepad icons may be corrupted so that instead of displaying their usual icon, which resembles a miniature Macintosh Plus, they revert to the standard generic document icon, which looks like a vertical piece of paper with the upper right-hand corner folded forward; and

- Inspection with a tool such as *ResEdit* or packages that can show invisible files reveals two such files in the System Folder named Scores (hence the name of the virus) and DeskTop.

Once the virus was detected, reverse engineering was applied by programmers to determine what it does and how it works.[13] They found that the virus lies dormant for various periods of time after infecting a host system, then performs certain functions. After two days, it begins to spread to other applications. After four days, the second part of the virus begins to watch for resources of type ERIC and VULT. If it finds such resources in a running application, it causes a system crash. After seven days, the virus causes frequent system crashes whenever applications containing ERIC and VULT resources are running and they attempt to write to disk.

Although the investigators have published detailed information on a way to detect and eradicate the disease, the process is not one you'd likely want to try. The virus is extremely contagious and will infect things such as *ResEdit*, that might be used to examine it. Fortunately, several antiviral agents have been

---

[11]See the definitions of worms and virus in the Glossary.

[12]If you read this sentence aloud to someone who doesn't know what you're reading from, the reaction should underline for you why the human disease analogy for computer viruses has been so popular.

[13][INFOMac], Volume 6, nos. 40 (23 April 88), 43 (26 April 88), and 46 (4 May 1988).

developed (see the Appendix for reviews of some). These are reasonably successful at detecting and eradicating SCORES, but you may still have to restore previously infected applications from your original master disks.

There has been some speculation that this virus was an attempt to attack programs developed by Electronic Data Systems (EDS) of Dallas.[14] Whatever the motivation and perpetrator (both still unknown), the virus was designed to attack programs with creator or type ERIC and VULT, and these identifiers apparently were used by EDS for proprietary internal programs at one time.

Unfortunately for everyone else, SCORES turns out to attack other programs as well. It's stable enough not to do this too often, so unless you had copies of the programs SCORES is designed to attack, you could spread the virus without realizing it's on your system. No one knows how many copies of SCORES are out there. It's been spread in several ways, including as a Trojan Horse: It was included with copies of a data compression program, apparently without the knowledge of the compression program's developer. Outbreaks of SCORES have been reported from several locations in the United States. EDS itself reported 24 infected machines on April 19, 1988.

MacMag Virus

We've already described the spread of the *MacMag* virus. Unfortunately, the extremely rapid and wide spread of this virus has opened the floodgates: The potential vandal now knows how easy it is.

Developed under the auspices of Richard Brandow, the publisher of *MacMag* magazine, and Drew Davidson, the *MacMag* virus is a time bomb designed to infiltrate its way through systems files and applications, reproducing as it goes. When these diseased programs are launched on a clean system, they proceed to infect that system. When the virus detects that the system clock indicates a date of March 2, 1988, it displays a "universal message of peace" from the staff of *MacMag*. It then removes itself from the system.

We have not received any reports of the virus damaging or destroying files, but some users have reported that its presence has caused certain applications to fail, causing the system to crash.

Aldus Corporation, which has incurred the loss of reputation involved in delivering copies of software infected with the *MacMag* virus, and the expenses of helping customers deal with the problem and of rebuilding Aldus' reputation, might take issue with a description of this virus as "benign."

---

[14]See [Cortino 1988].

PLO Virus

The PLO virus, discovered at the Hebrew University in Jerusalem, is an example of what some people have started to call a "political" virus. The virus wasn't too smart; it reproduced so often that it began to have noticeable effects on storage space. Also, rather than hiding long enough to spread really widely, it caused the computer it was on to slow down to about one-fifth of its normal speed half an hour after being switched on. It was set to go off (in this case, to destroy all accessible files) on Friday, May 13, 1988, the 40th anniversary of the last day Palestine existed as an independent country. The perpetrator has not been found, but the date and the fact of an attack on Israeli computer systems led to the name PLO virus and the notion of political virus programs.

BRAIN

BRAIN is an especially tricky DOS virus that surfaced recently at Miami University. The original strain is relatively benign and announces itself by changing the volume name of diskettes that include it to "(c) BRAIN". It was devised by software developers in Pakistan who wished to interfere with non-authorized copies of their programs; if you don't have such a pirate copy, all it should do is use up a bit of storage space. But mutations have been reported that are less benign, and it's easy to imagine a trivial modification that would not announce itself by changing the volume name when it infects a diskette. BRAIN is more insidious than some viruses because it infects systems through code inserted into the boot sector of the diskette; this code is executed and copies BRAIN at system load time, before any virus-protection programs that might be loaded from AUTOEXEC.BAT or CONFIG.SYS. BRAIN infects any diskette for which you ask DOS to show a DIRectory.

One of the things that makes BRAIN-type viruses especially dangerous is their ability to hide themselves. BRAIN stores itself in places like parts of your diskette marked as bad sectors, and actively protects itself against standard utilities that might look for it.

We've heard reports of a variation on BRAIN that infects Macintosh systems, but we haven't actually seen one.

SEX.EXE

SEX.EXE is a lot like Monkey-on-Your-Back, only for IBM and compatible computers. After you download the program and run it, the screen displays some rather interesting pictures of people doing interesting things. While you watch, the program copies its included virus into your system. Some time later, depending on how often you use the system utilities, the virus garbles the File Allocation Table on your hard disk.

There's a report of a Trojan Horse that does this on the Macintosh, with better graphics. As reported, it doesn't seem to reproduce itself, so it may not be a true virus.

nVIR Virus

Early in March 1988 came reports of the nVIR virus on the Macintosh. A symptom was unexplained system beeps when starting applications. Further investigation has shown that the virus installs several nVIR type resources in the application, and also modifies the CODE 0 resource and installs an INIT 32 resource. These changes have been reported in application as well as system files.

The virus appears to have three variants:

- The first version simply beeps when an application is started, but not every time and not for every application;
- A second version attempts to open *MacinTalk* and say "Don't Panic;" and
- The most destructive version randomly selects a file in the System Folder and destroys that file.

The first two variants are reported to be more virulent than the third and overwrite the third. All three variants can cause system crashes when launching an application (this is the only time the virus actually runs). There has been speculation that the variants may be different stages of the same virus or attempts by software vandals to build on each others' efforts. Antiviral agents have been developed for nVIR; see the Appendix.

HyperCard

In August, 1988, CompuServe and INFOMac reported to all subscribers that a virus was discovered in a *HyperCard* stack. This virus is written in *HyperTalk* code, the programming language used by *HyperCard* on the Macintosh. Once downloaded it replicates itself through other stacks on the user's system.

The virus prints this message:

Greetings from the HyperAvenger! I am the first HyperCard virus ever. I was created by a mischievous 14-year-old, and am completely harmless. Dukakis for president in '88. Peace on Earth and have a nice day.

The virus then replicates itself to the user's Home stack, and other stacks if it is not already there, and sets a timer for three weeks in the future when it will wake up again.

The virus claims to be harmless, and examination of the code tends to confirm this; however, there are three important observations:

1. The code for the virus is very simple when written in the *HyperTalk* language and may indeed have been developed by a 14 year old. This is not good news for Macintosh owners as a whole and is potentially catastrophic for HyperCard users for two reasons. First, HyperCard has the built in function of automatically updating changes to the disk without notifying the user. Second, in versions of HyperCard prior to version 1.2, there is no way for users to write-protect their stacks other than locking the physical disk, which can't be done on most Macintosh hard disks.

2. The present virus is annoying but apparently harmless. It could easily be modified to be dangerous and more virulent.

3. The message . . . Peace on Earth . . . suggests that the vandal who created this virus may have been motivated at least partly by the actions and resulting notoriety of the developers of the *MacMag* virus. The language and the tone of the displayed message offer a sad but pointed comment on the morality and social responsibility of the perpetrator.

NEW VIRUSES WITH NEW OPERATING SYSTEMS

New Exposures Match New Capabilities

The first real operating system for microcomputers was CP/M (Control Program for Microcomputers). It allowed people to make real use of the microcomputers then available, and for a short time was *the* operating system. The death knell for CP/M was DOS, combined with 8-bit processor chips. DOS allowed programmers to make use of things like 640K of memory (before, 16K was considered a lot of memory) and completely overwhelmed CP/M in the late 1970s and early 1980s. OS/2, or UNIX, or one of a small number of other candidates, repeatedly has been forecast to do the same for DOS in the late 1980s, by supporting fully the 16-bit and 32-bit processor chips. No one knows yet what operating system will be the eventual winner.

DOS won't die as quickly as CP/M did, simply because there are millions of DOS machines, and millions of people who aren't about to throw away billions of dollars worth of software and data. CP/M died quickly because there were only thousands, or hundreds of thousands at most, of CP/M machines.

What makes all this interesting in the context of computer viruses is that new viruses have come about for each new degree of capability of operating system. There weren't many (if indeed any) viruses in CP/M machines. DOS machines were relatively unaffected until communications and connectivity came into the picture. As system capabilities expand, it gets easier to spread viruses, the viruses (like any other program) can do more things, and with increasing interconnections things happen very fast. We believe that all new computers will soon have to spend some of their computing capability just making sure they don't get infected by a virus, or at least that they contain the damage.

MS-DOS and PC-DOS

With some 10 to 15 million copies of DOS, the most common microcomputer operating system, out there, it's clear that that system will be at the most risk. If nothing else, there simply are more of them. DOS (Disk Operating System) is provided with IBM and compatible computers. Today, DOS is the dominant micro operating system, with the Macintosh system that we look at later in second place at perhaps 1 to 2 million computers installed.

DOS comes in basically two versions: PC-DOS from IBM and MS-DOS from Microsoft. There are a few other minor variations, but everyone (except specialty users and a few other exceptions) either uses DOS or uses some operating system that looks the same to a program. A machine using DOS can be called IBM compatible, or PC compatible; we simply call it a DOS machine. Generally, the manufacturer of the machine makes no difference to a program, as long as it uses DOS.

As we said, several million machines out there use DOS. Thousands of programs have been written for DOS. Millions of person-years of spreadsheets, word processor files, accounting files and so on, reside in DOS. DOS for practical purposes is the same everywhere, which means that the same computer virus that attacks one DOS machine probably can attack every one of the other several millions just as successfully.

OS/2

For many months, OS/2 (the announced multi-user operating system for the newest generation of IBM personal computers) seems to have been vaporware. In late summer of 1988, it finally was possible to obtain a copy of the operating system;[15] however, there are only a few application programs written for it yet. The jury is out on the new operating system: A lot of people think it will take over from DOS within two or three years; many people think it won't. But for sure, viruses will develop along with applications; OS/2 is designed to fit in with the whole connectivity movement, which is what makes computer viruses a real pain rather than an obscure potential nuisance. OS/2, on the other hand, supports multiple users and has built-in security. It therefore may be less vulnerable than DOS for some of the same reasons minicomputer and mainframe operating systems have been.

Macintosh

The first Mac was introduced by Apple in early 1984, and programmers quickly discovered that the operating system was based on significantly different principles than other operating systems. Instead of issuing commands to perform a function, the user can select the action to be performed from a pull-down menu of options on the screen using a pointing device called a mouse. Users copy files by first clicking a button on the mouse while the arrow on the screen, which follows the movements of the mouse, points to a picture or icon of the file, and then selecting the "Duplicate" command from the menu. Duplicating an entire disk is even easier: You simply click on the icon of the disk to be duplicated and drag it on top of the icon of the disk to be written onto. Users never have to type arcane expressions like

```
copy a:\*.* b:\*.*  or
$duplicate gold:?.? ok
```

Life for users suddenly became much simpler, and thousands of people discovered computers through "the machine for the rest of us."

There was a price to be paid for all this added convenience and simplicity of operation: Programmers had to learn a vastly different way to write applications. To ensure that the standards Apple had so laboriously developed and implemented in the Macintosh were followed, programmers were required to develop programs that interfaced with the Mac operating system via a set of *ToolBox* routines built into the machine itself (see ROM in the Glossary). These routines, which are called whenever programmers wish to access some feature of the machine, act as an interface or translator between the programmer's application and the hardware. Since all Mac programs must use the *ToolBox*, they tend to do the same things the same way, at least as far as the user can tell.

---

[15]The original announced delivery date was around January 1987.

Common skills such as opening a file, saving a file, and selecting things learned from one program, usually transfer to other programs.[16]

What about viruses and Macs? Remember that a virus is a program--a series of instructions the computer has to execute. Because Macintosh viruses have to interact with the Mac system, vandals who wished to develop viruses on the Macintosh had to learn a new set of skills. This has meant that virus programs were rarer on the Macintosh than on other machines. At first, users had less to fear.

Unfortunately, this has changed. Since late 1987, viruses have surfaced on the Macintosh with growing frequency. The vandals appear to have learned their lessons well: Some of the viruses detected are quite sophisticated and run the gamut from "harmless" messages to potential industrial sabotage or revenge. (See "Some Famous Viruses" above.)

Along with this new crop of viruses, there have appeared antiviral products. Most of these are designed to detect one or more of the currently known viruses, and some attempt (with varying degrees of success) to remove the virus and/or to repair any damage caused. We discuss some of these products in the Appendix.

Viruses and Mainframe Systems

Oddly enough, virus programs have not been much of a problem in mainframe systems. In Chapter 1, we listed several reasons for this. Let's look at those more closely now.

Viruses and Timesharing

To be really technical, we should describe batch and interactive environments rather than mainframes and timesharing. That's not done here because all the mainframe systems you're ever likely to run across use both modes of operation. The greater risk by far is the interactive side of things, if only because there are thousands of people using the computer, often hundreds at the same time.

In the first place, each mainframe configuration is different from every other. Mainframes are generally found in very complex environments. It is not unusual to find thousands of users, each with a terminal or microcomputer and an account. There may be hundreds of peripherals attached to the computer itself, including many kinds of storage devices, printers, channel controllers,

---

[16]Trainers who work with both Macintosh and IBM personal computers have observed that novice students learn similar functions two to six times faster on the Mac than on other systems.

communications processors, and other devices. When the systems people start up a mainframe, they go through a process called a sysgen (from *system gener-ation*) during which they actually create the version of the operating system that will be installed. A potential virus can't simply assume that its target will be lo-cated at, say, byte number 1000, since the sysgen may have installed that part of the system somewhere else. This means that a virus that wants to attack another mainframe has to be much smarter: It has to be able to search for and find its target.

A second reason mainframes are less vulnerable is that their operating sys-tems are much more complex than microcomputer operating systems and were designed with the knowledge that there would be multiple users. One of the things designed into all multiple user operating systems is some form of security. You have to be able to protect users from each other, or the system will collapse. This protection means that it is much harder for a virus to move around and attack things. Microcomputer operating systems, on the other hand, usually don't contain any kind of security.

Another reason mainframe systems have fewer problems is implicit in our de-scription of the sysgen process: There are professionals around the shop. In fact, in most mainframe environments there are at least two people (with titles such as System Administrator, System Security Officer, and Database Administrator) who have training that includes how to find virus programs and the respon-sibility to do something about them.

Don't assume mainframes have no problems, however. Their operating systems can be penetrated (the list in the next section is from a mainframe operating system textbook). It's just that the methods used aren't the same. Users of a mainframe system are exposed to *each other* even if they're not at much risk from others outside the system. This could mean many thousands of people in a typical mainframe environment.

For one thing, any one of these people could decide to sabotage another user, or the system itself, and the vandal might use a virus to accomplish the vandalism. Even though people outside that system may not be at much risk, some thousands of users are exposed.

For another, a program for a micro is the same as any other data file to the mainframe. Since the mainframe is not at risk from the file, there is nothing to stop someone from using the mainframe to *spread* a virus from one micro to another micro. This happens all the time. If you read between the lines about viruses reported on mainframe computers, it turns out that the mainframe usually is serving merely as a transmission path and isn't itself infected. This seems to be the case for the PLO virus, for example; the virus infected Amiga computers that received files from a mainframe.

The introduction of microcomputers, and their use as terminals to connect to timesharing systems, has opened up several new avenues of risk. Unlike a "dumb terminal," a microcomputer can download things, change them, then upload them again. This is one way to spread a virus. Also unlike a dumb terminal, the microcomputer has programs of its own: A virus in a program on the mainframe might affect the programs in the micro. Again, we see that what makes computer virus programs more than a minor annoyance is the connectivity that lets them spread so far and so fast.

Perhaps the greatest threat of virus propagation in mainframes in the future will be through the use of UNIX and the C programming language. As part of the connectivity phenomenon, this language and operating system are migrating up to mainframes as well as down to micros. This means that already a virus that attacks UNIX may affect micros, minis, and mainframes. This kind of connectivity effect will increase.

TROJAN HORSES, SALAMIS, AND OTHER COMPUTER DELIGHTS

Computer virus programs are not the only risks computer users have to think about. Doing nasty things with or to computers is nothing new. That sort of thing has been happening for so long that there are lists of the most common penetration methods (a virus is one, naturally). Here, in fact, is a list of some of the favorite ways people have figured out for attacking computer systems.[17] Most of them even have names.

1. Between lines: A special terminal is used to tap into the communication line used by a legitimate user while the user is not active. Since a terminal user spends most of his or her time not active (e.g., thinking, or the time between keystrokes, or reading a screen display), there's room for someone to sneak in *between lines* with messages that look to the computer as though they come from the legitimate user.

2. Browsing: The user searches through the computer system, or files, attempting to locate sensitive information. Ideally, your system would not allow people to look at, say, password tables.

---

[17]Adapted from Fites, Philip, Martin Kratz, and Alan Brebner, *Control and Security in Computer Information Systems*, W. H. Freeman/Computer Science Press, 1988.

3. Traffic analysis: Similar to browsing, someone looks at things like how often you contact people, whom you contact, and what time of the day or week your contacts are. Quite a lot of information about what you're up to can be deduced from traffic analysis--and without alerting you by trying to intercept or change anything.

4. Denial of use: The user is able to crash the system, or hang it up by putting a program into an endless loop. The accidental virus described in Chapter 1 caused denial of the system to anyone else, as did the IBM Christmas card referred to earlier.

5. Hidden code: Programs may contain undocumented code that does things other than what is described in the manuals. Examples are viruses and worms. Other kinds of hidden code can be put into programs, with results that could be as drastic as a virus.

6. Interrupts: A penetrator may *cause* program or system interrupts; some operating systems allow such a user to enter a privileged mode with more access than usual, while processing an interrupt.[18] This can give the penetrator access to more capabilities than he normally would have.

7. Line disconnect: The user signs off, or the line goes down, but the system has not yet acknowledged and terminated the user's session. Until this termination occurs, another user may be able to use the session. A terminal or microcomputer that can do between-lines penetration probably also can do this one.

8. Masquerade: The penetrator obtains identification and passwords and signs on with someone else's account. A user pretending to be someone else by the line-disconnect or between-lines methods are forms of masquerade.

9. Operator deception: A penetrator may, for example, convince an operator to divulge a password (perhaps by claiming to have just changed the password and miskeyed the new one).

10. Piggyback: The penetrator intercepts a communication line and substitutes his or her own messages to the legitimate user and/or the system. For example, someone may simulate the signon program and thus get the user to give out identification and password information.

---

[18]This is a technical area and beyond the scope of this book. It doesn't apply as much to microcomputer systems; you're *always* in a privileged mode in a single-user microcomputer operating system. On multi-user systems especially, some kinds of program errors can kick a program into a "supervisor" or "privileged" mode. If this is not controlled extremely carefully, it can be--and has been--a way to penetrate complex mainframe operating systems.

11. Salami technique (not strictly an operating system penetration, but a well-known fraud):[19] The classic example is a program that accumulates all roundoff figures for a bank's loan calculations into one account. When each amount is rounded to an even penny, there will be small amounts left over.[20] Each such "slice" is less than 1/2 cent and is not noticeable, but for thousands of accounts the cumulative effect can be large.

12. Trojan horse: This is a generic name for a penetration method that includes hidden code. Something is in a program that is not supposed to be there, which causes sensitive data to be available; or, the program does not do what it is supposed to (Figure 2.5). It is possible to put a Trojan horse into a system that would, for example, simulate the logon messages: After collecting user identification data, the Trojan Horse would put the data somewhere accessible to the perpetrator and then remove itself from the system (this would be a masquerade). Familiar kinds of Trojan Horses in microcomputers are the freeware or shareware disk compression utility that spreads a virus as well as compresses data on your disk, and many computer games.

---

[19]See, for example [Krauss 1979].

[20]This is a well-known kind of fraud, but it is still seen from time to time. Financial institutions, by the way, are checked by regulators to be sure they don't accumulate all those roundoff errors into the *bank's* account, thus protecting consumers. Standard mathematical techniques are used to ensure that these unavoidable roundoff errors cancel each other out, rather than accumulating *anywhere*.

Figure 2.5 Trojan Horse

WHAT'S COMING NEXT?

What's coming next are vandals who will develop new viruses, and others who will develop new programs to fight them. There will be legal prosecutions, some of which will fail because sometimes the applicable laws can't handle things like a computer virus or the prosecutors are not familiar with this new form of crime. We'd like to think that one of the things that will happen is that viruses and similar attacks on computers will come to be seen as *vandalism*, and once people understand what is going on, they will stop admiring the Robin Hood image of the lone genius and recognize that spreading computer viruses is vandalism that's no better than slashing tires on cars for fun.

That's for the future. What you need to know is what's coming *now*. Unfortunately, we're very early in the cycle of attack and response, which means that you'll find a lot of new viruses soon. There's even a virus-creating program that is actually menu driven; that means even if you don't have the technical skills, you can still create a virus. There are at least two places where actual program code for a virus has been published. There's no special reason to think there won't be more.

Another thing that's coming next, and rather quickly, is greater connectivity. The information revolution is in full swing. The UNIX operating system is migrating from the minicomputers where it was developed up to mainframes and down to microcomputers. Manufacturers of computer hardware and software are competing to meet our needs for more and more access to other computers and for sharing data and programs. It's this sharing and access that makes it possible for a virus to infect many people's systems and to spread like wildfire.

Our advice is to assume that you are exposed and practice safe hex. Follow the pointers in this book to reduce your risk. Although you can't reduce your risk to zero (at least not without opting out of the information revolution), you can cut your risk greatly by adopting a few common-sense practices. Many commentators have used AIDS as an analogy. People aren't going to stop having sex--but practicing safe sex limits the ability of the HIV virus to spread. Practicing safe hex limits the ability of *computer* viruses to spread.[21]

Remember that others are aware of the virus problem too. After the experience of Aldus Corporation, every software developer is most likely reviewing its practices and procedures to ensure it doesn't get caught. Viruses had not been considered much of a problem until early 1988; now we all know better. Also, quite a few people have developed or are developing programs that search out known viruses, allow you to protect yourself from infection, or allow you to stop viruses from doing nasty things to your system. If everyone does his or her part, viruses will settle down to being a minor nuisance after a while. It's likely to get kind of interesting for a bit until things *do* settle down, though.

---

[21]Some writers have used the AIDS analogy to compare shrink wrap on program diskettes to condoms. Be warned: The analogy is very good indeed, including the fact that neither is 100% effective on its own. Another analogy is smallpox, which spreads by casual contact and was eradicated using practices similar to the sort we recommend for computer usage. (Like all analogies, this breaks down if carried too far; for example, AIDS and computer viruses mutate, smallpox doesn't.)

Chapter 3

WHAT CAN A VIRUS DO TO MY SYSTEM?

The day has arrived! I've reproduced myself fifty times and it's Friday the 13th. Now, let's look at that code over there--in the nasty ideas section--and see what I'm supposed to do.

Fortunately, a computer virus is simply a computer program. It's a virus because it attaches itself to other programs and reproduces itself; but foremost it's a computer program. That means it can only do what any other program can do, once it finds whatever condition it was designed to see as a trigger to start up. It also means there's no more limit on what a virus could do than there is on what any other program can do. Both are limited by your available memory and the pieces attached to your computer. But a malicious virus may do things no other program would consider, things that can actually destroy your computer.

THINGS VIRUSES HAVE DONE

•Fill up your computer with garbageware.[1]

A virus reproduces. And every copy of the virus takes up space somewhere. Moreover, all that space is space you can't use for your own legitimate purposes. The virus can fill up your disk, or your available memory, with copies of itself. Or perhaps just with zeros.

•Mess up files.[2]

---

[1][Computer Virus #1]

[2][Computer Virus #1]

As we'll see in Chapter 5, computer files are stored in standard ways. Therefore, it's very easy to alter things so that parts of files can't be located, even though they may still be there.

•Mess up the FAT.[3]

The FAT, or the File Allocation Table, contains information about where things are stored on your disk, as well as other information. Changing some of these items of information can cause you no end of grief.

•Mess up the boot sector.[4]

The boot sector is a special bit of information on a disk. If it's altered, your computer may not be able to run at all.

•Format a disk or diskette.[5]

A virus could simply format your disk, the same way you can with a FORMAT or initialize command.

•Display a message.[6]

The *MacMag* virus just displayed a message, harmlessly. So could any other virus. But the message need not be harmless: Consider obscenities scrawled on computer screens as they are now spray painted onto walls.

•Put messages into printouts.[7]

A virus could also add messages to printer output. This could be more than slightly annoying if, for instance, the virus put obscenities into several hundred form letters.

•Reset a computer.[8]

You can press several keys that will reset your computer. A virus could send the same codes to the operating system, which would be annoying, to say the least.

---

[3][Computer Virus #1]

[4]Documentation for typical antiviral software; for example *NTIVIRUS* from Orion Microsystems.

[5][Computer Virus #2]

[6][Computer Virus #2]

[7]Conversation with Dr. H. Highland.

[8]Conversation with an antiviral product developer.

•Slow things down.[9]

> Most programs are written to run as *fast* as possible. You can also write programs to be deliberately *inefficient*. A virus could really slow things down for you.

•Redefine keys.[10]

> Your computer has to be told what a signal from the keyboard means. A virus could change the definitions in the keystroke definition table.

•Lock the keyboard.[11]

> If the virus deleted the keyboard definitions, the computer would not respond at all.

•Change data in programs or files.[12]

> Some viruses have made random changes to data files, and you might not notice this for a long time. Even worse, they could change random data in memory (RAM), causing erratic program results. The evidence goes away when you reload the program to fix the problem.

•Physically damage the hard drive or other parts of the machine.[13]

> There are several ways a program, a virus in this case, can cause actual physical damage to your machine. Some reported cases involve potential hazards to you as well as to the machine.

•Copy data you have access to for another user who shouldn't have access.[14]

> This type of problem applies mostly to systems with many users (e.g., time-sharing systems). If you have access to, say, payroll information or confidential medical records, a virus could copy it to a place where someone else without your access level can get at it.

---

[9][Computer Virus #1]

[10][Computer Virus #2]

[11]If you can redefine keys, you can lock the keyboard by setting up an empty keystroke definition table.

[12][Computer Virus #2]

[13][Computer Virus #3]

[14]Some of the National Security Agency's material on microcomputer security covers this sort of exposure; it's not too significant for most microcomputer users who don't work with military or national security systems.

Don't be too frightened about this list. Remember a virus does *nothing* to your system unless it *runs*. If you don't run programs containing viruses, they don't spread, and no damage is done.

Chapter 4

HOW GREAT IS MY EXPOSURE?

Now, where should I go to find my next victim? Let's see, what's the easiest thing to get at? Oh, nuts; that's a read-only communications line, I can't get down it. Over there--well, really, you can't expect me to go after a single micro like that when I can get at this other BBS, and reach a lot of micros!

Don't let the virus scare stop you from joining in the connectivity revolution. If you do, your exposure to computer virus programs is minimal. But you also deny yourself the incredible benefits available by sharing programs, ideas, and so on with other computer users. Therefore, take some chances; but also practice safe hex to control your exposure to viruses.

PIRATE SOFTWARE

When you use pirate copies of software (that is, copies you didn't pay for), you're accepting software from someone who knowingly violated the law. Do you want to assume that that person is too moral to insert a virus into the stolen software? And can you assume that he or she is careful enough to be sure of the source? Tom Keenan of the University of Calgary said it best, "You have to be careful what you pick up in the gutter."[1]

BULLETIN BOARDS AND OTHER COMMUNICATIONS

Bulletin boards present the greatest exposure to computer viruses. There are thousands of BBSs. Most of them have freeware and shareware programs available for downloading. And some manufacturers distribute product fixes

---

[1][Graham 1988]

and upgrades on BBSs. If you're simply a user of microcomputers, along with the several million others, your greatest risk probably is downloading from a BBS (Figure 4.1). Check out the suggestions in Chapter 7 and elsewhere.

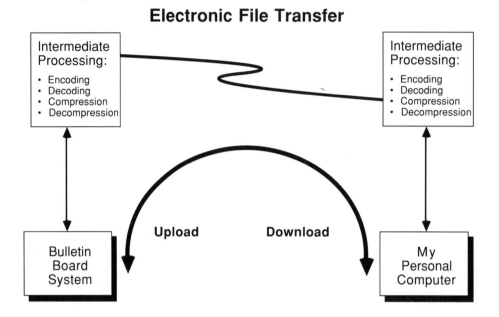

Figure 4.1 Uploading and Downloading Programs

People who download and try out many games are especially at risk. Games change frequently, have a short lifetime, and are a common and enjoyable form of sharing neat ideas with other computer users. Unfortunately, these very characteristics mean that viruses are easy to include, and hard to detect. People who use programs masquerading as useful utilities for disk and data compression are also at significant risk, since many of these programs have been reported to contain viruses. These are popular because many BBSs store and transmit programs in compressed data formats (to save space and transmission time) (Figure 4.2). This means that you have to run the de-compression program to try out the program; thus if the compress/de-compress program is infected it gets a chance to infect anything else you might upload or download. Disk compression or reorganization programs are popular as well, and since they are intended to work with parts of your system that viruses often attack, the action of the virus is masked until it's too late for you to stop it. At least one antiviral program has been reported to spread a virus of its own.

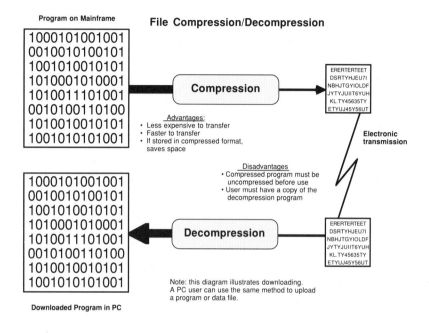

Figure 4.2 Compression and Decompression

In preparing this book, we downloaded programs from bulletin boards in various places. We suggest you practice safe hex as we did. Don't download unless you can verify the credentials of the BBS operators. We consider major public domain BBSs such as CompuServe or various publications' BBS operations, or BBSs where we know the operators personally or can contact them and verify their credentials, to be pretty safe (*not* perfectly safe). When you contact operators, find out what they're doing to keep their own environments safe and sterile. If they do nothing, don't telephone their bulletin boards. If they're aware of the exposures and have a reasonable program, you can consider them reasonably safe. Avoid any BBS that allows downloading of proprietary software; why assume their morality about viruses is better than about copyright violations?

We checked every so-called "vaccine" we downloaded with every tool available, including some trusted antiviral programs. We looked at each program file to be sure there weren't any interesting "HA HA GOTCHA" type text strings. Then we tested each new program on a separate system with no connection to our normal working systems.[2] This might be overkill for you. We were careful, and we were downloading things that are known to be risky. We recommend that you be careful too, especially if you also download things known to be risky.

ELECTRONIC MAIL

It's been reported that at least one virus has spread through an electronic mail (e-mail) system. You sign on, read your mail (that is, copy a message and maybe something else from the mail system into your own computer), and *voila!* you have been infected. We haven't been able to verify this report, and it may be simply a scare story. The known e-mail problems (the IBM Christmas card, for instance) may not even be programs, let alone viruses.[3] It's perfectly possible for an unusually high level of otherwise normal activity to fill up all available space in an electronic mail system.

We have a bit of difficulty imagining how a virus that piggybacked on an e-mail message could get itself activated. Many e-mail systems don't even allow transmission of anything other than ASCII text (the kind of normal characters you type on the keyboard), and you wouldn't try to execute ASCII text files[4] (not twice, anyway). We'd be much more cautious about an e-mail system or bulletin board system allowing transfer of executable files (see the previous section).

SABOTAGE BY EMPLOYEES

Sabotage by employees is one of the standard computer security exposures. Employees have access to your system, as well as training in using at least the part of the system needed for their job. Unhappy employees (or former employees) have tried to sabotage computer systems to get even. The SCORES virus, for

---

[2]When we did this, we didn't find any *known* viruses, but a *new* one came along with a "protection" program and infected the test system.

[3]There's uncertainty about the IBM Christmas card. Some have reported it as a virus, but technically, we might call it a worm rather than a virus. It may not even have been a program; it takes a lot of storage to save a high-resolution color screen image, and too many copies of something like that will fill up the available storage for any mail system. See also Chapter 2.

[4]There are programs that can map the non-ASCII characters found in program code or formatted word processing or spreadsheet files into and back from ASCII. This is not the sort of thing you'd do by accident, since you must run programs at both ends to do such translation/decoding. If you don't do something like that, e-mail messaging normally won't pose an exposure.

example, may have been an attempt by an ex-employee against the former employer.

Another situation in which employee sabotage is common is labor disputes. If you are the security manager for a company with any possibility of a labor dispute, be extremely careful about viruses and logic bombs. Imagine, for example, a logic bomb going off in a program controlling a catalytic cracker in a refinery; the damage could be millions or more, including loss of human life.

TERRORISM

Frankly, we consider *all* viruses outside of research laboratories to be instances of terrorism. That aside, there are many *real* terrorist groups in the world--the Red Brigade, the Japanese Red Army, the Palestine Liberation Organization, the Irish Republican Army, among others. These groups do things like bomb airports, hijack planes, and kill innocent tourists, all attacks against innocent civilian targets. The Red Brigade manifesto specifically includes destruction of computer systems as an objective.[5] In Japan, at least one group messed up the control lines (computerized) for commuter trains, paralyzing a major city for several hours. The PLO virus at Hebrew University may have been an instance of political terrorism.

We can't be too optimistic about this exposure. All we can say for sure is that practices that reduce your risk to viruses in general help whether the virus is planted by a terrorist or simply some ordinary vandal with technical skills and no morals.

INDUSTRIAL ESPIONAGE

In an ideal world, companies would compete only by producing better products at better prices and making them more available to consumers. Our world isn't ideal. There are reports of companies trying to spy out each others' secrets. From time to time, the business press reports that someone has actually sabotaged another company. This can be done in many ways. Extortion by threats of poisoning things like candy bars or drug capsules has happened. A few instances have been reported where employees (current or former) have done things like encrypt important data and demand ransom in return for the

---

[5][Bruschweiler 1985]

encryption key. A virus program could be another method of extortion.[6] When this kind of thing is done by unethical companies or individuals it's called industrial espionage or industrial sabotage or simply extortion.

The *MacMag* virus infected a commercial software vendor's products; the diskettes in shrink wrap contained a virus.[7] The vendor recalled all infected products, at considerable cost. This was an unintended side effect of a benign virus. It could have been an intentional instance of industrial sabotage.

A virus also could be inserted into a network. If carefully constructed, the virus could replicate and spread for quite a while before being discovered. If it spread widely enough, it might be impossible to eradicate the virus completely from the network.[8] Suppose, for example, a virus in your company's computer network did nothing other than copy your latest budget figures into the computer system of your largest competitor. This would be an example of virus used for industrial espionage.

FINANCIAL SYSTEMS

Financial systems will always face special risk: That's because they deal in money. If you can get into their systems, potentially you can get at a very large amount of money at computer speeds. (This has happened several times already, although not yet by using viruses).[9] It's been speculated in the computer trade press that one penetration method could be via the employees' microcomputers and a virus.[10]

---

[6]See, for instance, articles on computer abuse in the May-June 1988 issue of *The Computer Law and Security Report*.

[7]The exact infection path hasn't been made public. The process of manufacturing software includes program development and testing and actual duplication of production diskettes. Often, the duplication is done by a specialist other than the actual developer. There are many points of attack where a virus could get into a program diskette before it's shrink wrapped. For that matter, shrink wrap is easy enough to apply, and someone could break the package, infect the program, then shrink-wrap the infected program. The major developers are very aware now of these exposures, and some of them have taken steps already.

[8]What do you do when all your backups, as well as your current files, are infected? You can avoid new infection by encryption and other means, but this doesn't get rid of existing infections. Of course, you can shut the network down and start over, but that may be very expensive.

[9]At least not yet reported.

[10]The emphasis is on *could be*. There are many reasons why this probably wouldn't work.

A less obvious commodity that financial institutions deal in is trust. You trust your bank's computers.[11] What would you think if you found out that a virus has infected them? Would you leave your money in that bank? There's an opportunity here for industrial sabotage as well as simple bank robbery.

MILITARY AND NATIONAL SECURITY ESPIONAGE

The entire military and national security area is very specialized and outside the scope of this book. Others are looking into viruses here; there are reports that the National Security Agency in the United States has hundreds of people working on the problem of protection against viral infection, for example. Since you're not directly involved or likely to be at risk, we suggest that you save this area for interesting speculations and movies.[12]

---

[11]We are less trusting, having too good an idea of how fallible computer systems are. We urge you to reconcile your checkbook and credit card statements and *not* to assume the error is yours if there's a discrepancy.

[12]The movie *War Games* has this as its theme, as do many science-fiction books. You might enjoy John Brunner's *Shockwave Rider*; Spider Robinson's *Mindkiller*; Greg Bear's *Eon*; or E. E. Smith's Family D'Alembert series, especially #10, *Revolt of the Galaxy*.

Chapter 5

FOR TECHIES ONLY: WHAT IS A VIRUS *REALLY?*

Oh, oh. Is that an electronic microscope they're pointing at me? Even a virus be-
comes visible when you look closely enough.

As we have said, a virus is a computer program that replicates itself by attaching itself to other programs, and then performs some non-documented function (usually nasty). Most viruses make their way into a system by using a variation of a Trojan Horse (a program that does one thing, usually nifty, while also releasing the virus into your system). That's a nice definition, but what does it mean on a more basic, nuts and bolts level? This chapter presents relatively technical information about how DOS and the Macintosh work and how viruses infect them. We also take another look at BBSs with the technical material in the first part of the Chapter 5 as a base.

ANATOMY OF A VIRUS

So far, our virus is rather simple; Figure 5.1 is a flowchart for it. This flowchart is missing a thing or two; most viruses are more complex than that. Each chapter of this book begins with an example of the sort of thing that might be happening inside a "thinking" virus; we'll use that virus as an example to show how viruses can be created. Keep in mind, however, that this is not the only way a virus can be created. It is just a sample to show the kinds of things that normally are included. Our particular virus is a DOS virus, although the same basic logic would work in other operating systems. Figure 5.2 is a flowchart for our virus. Note that each box in the figure has a number; the step numbers in the text correspond to these box numbers. Now here's how our thinking virus works.

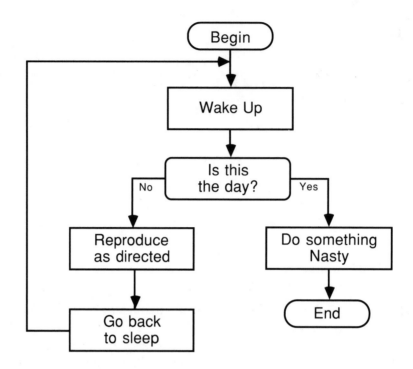

Figure 5.1 A Simple Virus

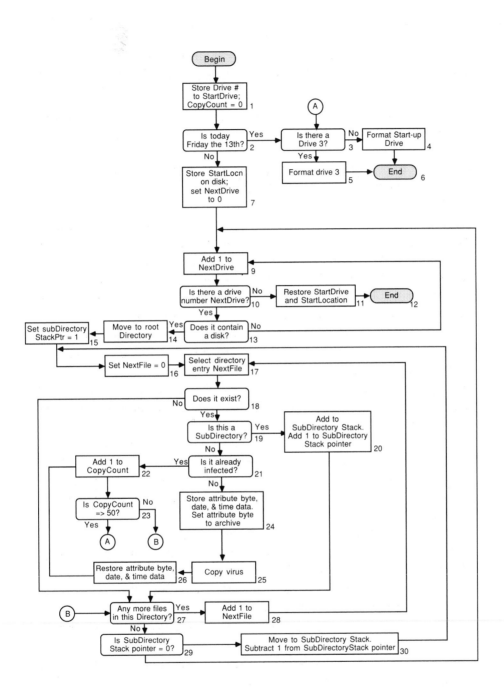

Figure 5.2 A More Complex Virus

This virus has problems, by the way. For one thing, it's slow. For another, the process involved would cause a large amount of activity for the disk drive light; even a non-paranoid user might get rather suspicious.

Step 1 Figure out where we are and save the information. We will need this information later. Also, set the count of how many copies of the virus we have found to 0.

Step 2 Is this The Day? If it is, then go to our "do something nasty" subroutine. If not, then get on with the business of reproducing.

Step 3 to *Step 6* This group of steps is the actual logic bomb part of the virus. Format the hard drive, usually the third drive on a system (drive C). If there is no hard drive, format the drive we started on. Once that is done, we can quit. There is no need to tell the victim about our presence; the person will realize it the next time he or she tries to boot the system.

Step 7 If this is not the day, store our location on the current drive (which subdirectory are we in?) so we can return when we're done.

Step 8 Initialize our variable for the drive we are working on. This marks the beginning of the outermost loop of our structure. This loop will move us through the available drives on the target system.

Step 9 to *Step 14* Find the next drive in sequence. If there is no next drive, we're finished, since DOS won't allow systems to skip numbers when assigning drives. If there is a next drive, is there a disk in it? If not, start this group of steps again. If there is a disk, move to it, then move to its root directory.

Step 15 Initialize the pointer to the top of the directory stack. This pointer will be used to keep track of which subdirectory we are going to work on next. Then begin the second loop, which will move us through each sub-directory in turn.

Step 16 Initialize the file pointer. It will be used to keep track of which file in the current directory we are presently working with. Then begin the third loop, which moves us through each file on the current directory.

Step 17 to *Step 19* Select the file to be worked on. Make sure it's not an erased file, and determine if it's a subdirectory.

Step 20 If it's a subdirectory, add its position to the subdirectory stack and increment the stack pointer.

Step 21 to *Step 22* Make sure the file is not already infected. If it is, add 1 to the count of how many copies we've found.

Step 23 If the count is 50 or more, go to the nasty routine in Steps 3 to 6.

Step 24 If the file is not infected, save the system telltales and the attribute byte for the file. Set the attribute byte to Hex '00' to make the file "normal" and allow unlimited access.

Step 25 Copy the virus into place. (As explained in Chapter 1, this is not a book about how to create viruses. We've therefore chosen to omit certain details in this flowchart, and this is one such area.)

Step 26 Cover our tracks so that no one will notice what we have done. Restore the system telltales and attribute byte to the way they were before we did our thing. When we've finished reproducing, add 1 to the copy count and check to see if the count is over 50 and we're supposed to blow up.

Step 27 to *Step 28* Are there any more files here? If there are, increment the file pointer and start the third loop again.

Step 29 to *Step 30* Is there another subdirectory in the stack? If so, move there, pop the stack, and start the second loop again. If not, we are finished with disk, so start the main loop again.

(The exits from this procedure are in *Steps 6* and *12*.)

TARGETS

Generally, a virus has a target cell--a program or area it has been designed to attack--and a target site--a place it has been designed to hide until it attacks its target cell. These targets vary depending on the operating system the machine uses. We will look at the two most common microcomputer operating systems, DOS[1] and the Apple Macintosh. If your machine uses another operating system such as UNIX or CP/M, a little research and common sense will give you a similar list of targets.

DOS

DOS is the most common microcomputer operating system, so we'll look at it first.

Target Sites

The target site is the entity that the virus program is designed to attack. This section looks at several common targets.

---

[1]For our purposes, the IBM version PC-DOS and the Microsoft version MS-DOS can be considered identical.

The Old Reliables

Some files are virtually guaranteed to exist on any DOS system. Whenever you enter a command, the DOS program COMMAND.COM looks at what you've entered and decides whether the command invokes a built-in DOS command, a .COM or .EXE file, a .BAT file, or a "BAD COMMAND OR FILE NAME." Therefore, most DOS machines have a COMMAND.COM file in the root directory; although it is possible to tell DOS to use another program that does more or less the same thing instead of COMMAND.COM, it is not a common occurrence. If this replacement were made, however, a CONFIG.SYS file would have to be present in the root directory of the boot disk. This is because the only way to replace COMMAND.COM is by a command contained in CONFIG.SYS (the SET COMSPEC= command). Since a COMMAND.COM or a CONFIG.SYS must be located in the root directory of the boot disk, many viruses target COMMAND.COM, CONFIG.SYS, or both.

Other files almost certain to exist in a DOS system are the system files supplied by Microsoft or IBM. These files, named IBMBIO.COM and IBMDOS.COM by IBM and IO.SYS and MSDOS.SYS by Microsoft, are set as system files, which means they are invisible. Don't panic if you don't find them; normal DOS utilities like DIR won't list these hidden files.[2] One or the other of these sets of files *must* be present in a DOS system. Their invisibility makes them prime targets, since you aren't likely to notice alterations to them.

Certain other files, such as standard DOS utilities like CHKDSK.COM and BACKUP.COM, also are likely to occur in a DOS system, and may be targeted.[3] Any AUTOEXEC.BAT file or CONFIG.SYS file also may be a target.

Time Bombs

One interesting place for a virus to hide itself is in the CMOS storage that keeps the setting of the system clock. An add-on board that uses a rechargeable battery to keep this setting while the computer is turned off is a very popular and inexpensive accessory. Because such clock boards are common, viruses may target the storage in them.[4]

Three things make this an especially dangerous type of virus. First, the clock is about the first thing run when the computer starts up and usually will be the

---

[2]The attribute byte is set to Hidden, System, Read-only, and Archive. The DIRectory command won't list any file that is marked hidden or as a system file.

[3]In fact, one precaution recommended is to change the names of some of these files; for example, change FORMAT to NEWDISK.

[4]Some newer machines such as the IBM AT and compatibles and the PS/2 series also store some parts of the operating system in another separate CMOS area. Macintosh computers also store certain data in CMOS.

first thing in an AUTOEXEC.BAT file.[5] Therefore, a virus in the CMOS can get into RAM, where it can run and do its replicating or damage, before any antiviral programs you may have can catch it. Second, a DIR (or a file utility) won't see this virus, since it's not a file in the usual sense. Finally, none of the common tools available for manipulating files can access the CMOS storage area.[6]

Catch as Catch Can

The two simplest ways to install a virus into your system are to attack executable files or to attack .BAT files. Any file that has the extension .EXE or .COM is considered executable (some viruses may also look for extensions like .OVL or .PGM that are used by specific programs). The virus attaches itself to the end of these files, and replaces the first function call in the program with a jump to the virus. It then inserts the function call just replaced at the end of the virus, so that the last thing the virus does is to begin apparently normal program execution.

For .BAT files, the virus might copy itself as a .COM file into a directory and set the attribute byte for that .COM file to hidden. It then adds a line to the .BAT file, which calls the hidden file. This is fairly easy to spot (if you look at the .BAT file), and fix: Delete the line, then use a utility that will see hidden files to delete the file.

The hardest virus to catch without using special programs is a TSR virus. A TSR (*Terminate and Stay Resident*) virus uses the same technique that a print spooler and other memory resident programs use. The program, or a virus, simply loads itself into RAM and stays there, waiting for an unprotected disk to be put into a drive. The virus then copies itself to the disk and does whatever else it is designed to do. About the only way you'll notice one of these viruses (unless you use a vaccine that traps TSR calls; see the Appendix) is when you notice there is less available memory (RAM) than usual. This may be difficult if you don't have special programs, since standard DOS utilities don't give you this information. If the virus is stored in the boot sector of a drive (see the next section) or in CMOS, you won't see it with any DOS file utility.

Remember that a virus has to be run, just like any other program, before it can reproduce itself or do anything to your system. Somewhere in the virus there has to be code that causes it to get itself run; the means listed above are some common, although not the only possible, ways.

---

[5]ATs, PS/2s, and Macintosh computers also load from CMOS first thing.

[6]See Chapter 8 for one way to diagnose and fix this situation.

Target Areas

This section looks at some of the more common places that viruses attack.

Devastating but Direct

Three of the most vital sections of any computer disk are the boot sector, the File Allocation Tables (FAT), and the root directory track. Unfortunately, these three areas are also among the most vulnerable to a virus attack. Such an attack can be, in a word, devastating.

The boot sector is the section of the disk that contains the instructions the computer uses to begin working. The instructions contain a bit of machine code that supports a read, or whatever else is needed to get the operating system loaded. The boot sector is always located in the same place on any disk and can't be accessed by any of the standard DOS utilities. Damage to the boot sector of a disk renders that disk unbootable. This is not a huge problem if the disk is a floppy diskette (and you have a backup), but it is a disaster if the disk is your hard disk. The result is that the system refuses even to acknowledge the physical existence of the hard drive, responding to all attempts to access it with INVALID DRIVE SPECIFICATION. In that case, the disk is gone. That is to say, it *cannot* be recovered; you will have to reformat it and restore programs and files from your backups.[7] (You *do* have current backups, don't you?)

The File Allocation Table (FAT) is the section of the disk that DOS uses to keep track of the clusters of storage space available for use by new files. Basically, DOS uses disk space as it becomes available, and the FAT tells DOS where the clusters associated with files named in the directory have been put on the disk (the physical location, as opposed to the logical location in the directory track).

The FAT contains the locations of the clusters used for each file and pointers so that the system knows which clusters each file uses and which clusters are available.[8] This method of managing storage is called a linked list by programmers (Figure 5.3).

---

[7]At least one of the antiviral programs on the market, *NTIVIRUS*, has features that sometimes overcome this problem; see the Appendix.

[8]You do wind up with pieces of files scattered all over the place after a while. Although the system will store new files, access slows down because the disk has to jump all over to find clusters. The popular compression programs reorganize the clusters so that they're all contiguous. Since such programs must access the FAT, a virus that might be concealed in them would be doing the same kind of thing the program is expected to do; you wouldn't have any idea that damage was being done until you tried to access things later.

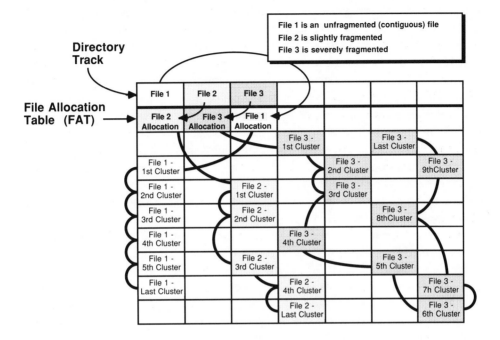

Figure 5.3 FAT: File Allocation Table

It is easy to see why the FAT is important to the computer system and why damage to it is so disastrous. Unfortunately, the FAT is quite vulnerable, since it always starts at the same location, Side 0 Sector 2, and FAT entry 0 always contains a three-digit hexadecimal number that describes the type of disk in use and the format for storage on that disk. Once these facts are known, a virus program always will know the length of the FAT and the location and maximum size of the root directory. This data can be modified at will. Imagine what it would be like to power up your machine and discover that the system now thinks your 40-megabyte hard disk is a single-sided, low-density floppy capable of storing only 160 kilobytes.

Since the FAT areas can be accessed only by an absolute read or an absolute write, which are special assembler level commands, the system is protected from accidental modification of the FAT. There are valid reasons for wanting to modify the FAT, however, and any good manual on advanced DOS programming techniques contains all the information needed by a competent system programmer.

Several antiviral programs and utilities on the market provide the ability to save a version of the FAT to protect against inadvertent damage (see the Appendix). Some of the utilities provide the capability to modify the FAT as well as other areas of the disk. These tools are very dangerous in the hands of unsophisticated users, and *extreme caution* must be exercised when using them. Improper use of these tools can mess up your disk just as badly as a virus could.

All DOS disks have a data storage area called a directory. The directory is a list of the files on the disk; it has a maximum number of entries, set at the time the disk is formatted. Before the appearance of affordable hard disks, this maximum number was not often a problem, since users usually ran out of space long before running out of available directory slots for entries. With increases in available disk space (e.g., hard disks, double and quad density diskettes), a solution to the problem of too many directory entries had to be found. With DOS 2.0, a special class of file called a subdirectory was introduced. The subdirectory acts like an extra directory, effectively squaring the number of files that can be put onto the disk. (If the directory could hold, say, 10 files, and one file is a subdirectory, then the total number of possible files would be 98: one hundred names, less two that are used up by the subdirectory and its name in the directory.) Since each subdirectory can contain files, and a subdirectory is itself a file, a subdirectory can contain another subdirectory; this means that the only limit to the number of files that can be stored is the space available on the disk.

Subdirectories are organized in what programmers call a tree structure (Figure 5.4). The original directory is called the root directory. All subdirectories contain two files in addition to the ones the user creates. These files show up as . and .. to the DOS DIRectory command. The .. file contains a pointer to the parent directory, the place where the subdirectory was created. The . file contains the list of files located in the subdirectory. To DOS, the root directory and the . file look more or less the same. Each contains the same information for each file it lists, including the name, extension, size, and starting FAT cluster.

All this lovely data about files makes a very tempting target for a virus. If even 1 byte is changed, whole directories can seem to disappear: The data are still there, but the system can't find them.

Altering or erasing an entry for a subdirectory does not actually destroy data, just the path the system uses to locate the data. Sometimes, you can "un-erase" a file or recover from certain kinds of damage with programs like CHKDSK.COM or some commercial utilities.

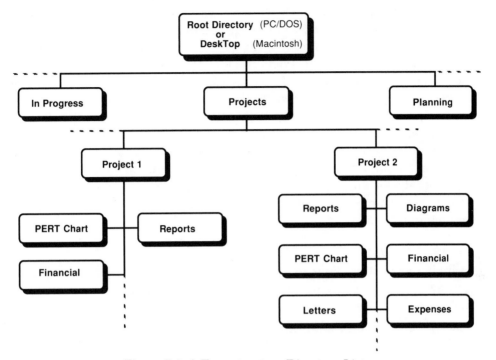

Figure 5.4 A Tree-structure Directory List

What Do You Mean "FILE NOT FOUND"

One of the less damaging types of virus (if you have backups) is the one targeted at a specific program or developer. Since most distribution copies of programs come write-protected, the original should be safe from infection. When you buy a program, it should come in a shrink-wrapped package. *Write-protect* your disk (cover the notch in the upper right-hand corner on a 5 1/4 inch diskette, or move the little plastic tab on a 3 1/2 inch diskette) *before* you put the disk into your computer for the first time. This is the best available way to ensure that at least one copy of the program stays free of disease.

Of course, a virus attack may be more subtle than simply erasing a file. A knowledgeable vandal may have the virus alter internal program settings, thus changing what the program does. You wouldn't know about the change until you ran across the function, by which time the virus could be pretty widespread. The fix is to restore the program from your clean copy and track down and eradicate the copies of the virus.

The real problem comes up when some other program happens to fit the profile of the target program for the virus (e.g., SCORES).

As noted in the previous section, erased files don't actually go away; they're simply marked with a code that indicates they're erased. If a program is erased and you haven't re-used the freed-up clusters, the file can be recovered by any of several available utilities. (Basically, they change the erased flag back to something else, thereby un-erasing the file. If you've written over one or more clusters, the utilities allow you to chase clusters and re-attach them.)

These utilities are extremely useful--*if you really know what you're doing*. If you don't, you can do so much damage that the whole disk becomes unusable. Also, in practice it often turns out that it takes longer to fix this kind of problem than to restore from your backups and re-enter the lost data. (You do have current backups, don't you?)

Now That's *Twisted*

Probably the most insidious form of virus is one that targets random bytes on your disk. A byte is selected at random, and changed to some random value. Figure 5.5 shows this effect.

The horrible thing about this is that you might not know what's happening for months. By that time the virus could have spread to who knows where. If the random byte were part of some word processing document, it likely would be attributed to human error. (One or two characters changed; someone made a typing error, right? Not necessarily.) If the random byte were part of a program, the results would be unpredictable. Either way, tracing the source would be extremely difficult.

One protection against such random changes is to use a checksum method and create a signature for each file. You apply some arithmetic to the file, perhaps also to the attribute byte, path, file name, and creation date, and compute a number, which you store. Then if anything changes, the signature will change and you can suspect a virus or some other error (and avoid trying to run the program). Several of the antiviral products listed in the Appendix offer this kind of capability. This does not protect you if you create a signature for an infected file, however.

A similar technique is to encipher program files. If a virus changes them, they won't decipher into anything useful. (Some utility packages such as *PCTOOLS* have limited capabilities for encryption. Sophisticated products are available in the area of security packages, but most are more comprehensive than needed for this purpose and many are rather expensive.) Encryption doesn't save your data

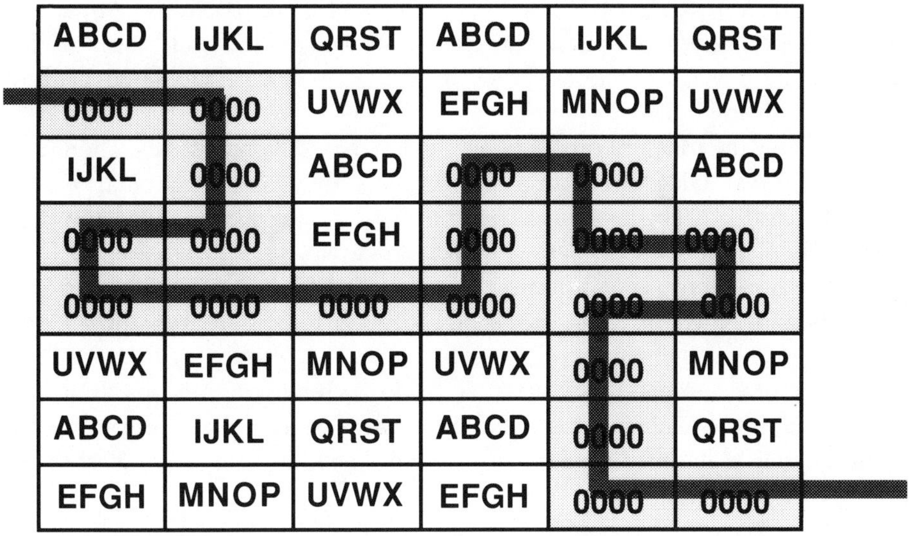

ABCD	IJKL	QRST	ABCD	IJKL	QRST
0000	0000	UVWX	EFGH	MNOP	UVWX
IJKL	0000	ABCD	0000	0000	ABCD
0000	0000	EFGH	0000	0000	0000
0000	0000	0000	0000	0000	0000
UVWX	EFGH	MNOP	UVWX	0000	MNOP
ABCD	IJKL	QRST	ABCD	0000	QRST
EFGH	MNOP	UVWX	EFGH	0000	0000

Figure 5.5 Altered Data

or programs, but it protects you from running a diseased program--again, if your file isn't already infected when you protect it. You could implement this through .BAT files.[9] Be careful not to lose the keys if you encrypt things. We think that encryption is a bit much, unless you are in a sensitive environment or are talking about things like password tables.

Macintosh

The Macintosh operating system is significantly different from DOS. From the users' viewpoint, it is mostly graphics-oriented, with few requirements to type commands. From the programmer's point of view, it is also very different. To understand how viruses work in Macintosh systems, you first have to know a bit about how the Mac works.

All calls issued by a program are routed through the *ToolBox* before being acted upon by the System. This helps ensure that programs will work the same on different Macintosh computers, even if the actual architecture of the machine or the System changes (presently there are seven variations: Mac 128, Mac XL (or

---

[9][Pozzo 1986] covers some technical details of this method of virus protection.

Lisa), Mac 512, Mac 512E, MacPlus, Mac SE, and Mac II). Basically, Apple has said that if programmers follow the rules and make their calls through the *ToolBox* in the approved manner, their programs will run the same on any Macintosh with any released system.

Programs on the Mac are organized as *resources* of different types: There is a resource type for dialog boxes, one for windows, one for object (binary) code itself, and so forth.[10] This has the effect of making a program modular and thus easier to modify and encourages a good top-down, structured approach to program construction. In addition, these resources can be copied from one application to another for re-use, local modification for different countries, and so on.

There is a programmers' tool available to do such copying and modification called *ResEdit*; it's available on many bulletin boards or from Apple through local dealers. Having mentioned *ResEdit*, we offer you the following heavy warning:

> *ResEdit* is a very powerful tool that will allow a programmer to access the inner workings of files on the Macintosh. It is assumed that users of *ResEdit* have an intimate knowledge of the Macintosh System, file structure, *ToolBox*, and so on. If you don't, and you try to use *ResEdit*, you are likely to seriously or fatally damage files. *ResEdit* is not for beginners.

If you do plan to dig around in the internals of programs, the single most important precaution you can take is always to work with a *copy* of the program. Once you have finished, *test* that copy thoroughly before trusting it, and only then replace the original--and keep a backup of the original just in case.

ResEdit is also an excellent tool for inspecting programs suspected of harboring disease. It's the way most investigations into the internal workings of Macintosh viruses are conducted. Most of the developers who have investigated viruses create a vaccine or other antiviral agent once they have identified the problem; many of these vaccines are discussed in the Appendix.

Several other tools are available, both commercially and as shareware, that allow capabilities similar to *ResEdit*. They also are not for beginners and must used with in-depth knowledge and great caution.

If you don't have a technical background, use vaccines such as those mentioned in the Appendix, rather than *ResEdit*, to fix your problem.

---

[10]For technical details, we recommend *Inside Macintosh*, Volumes I-V, Addison-Wesley; the *Macintosh Programmers' Workshop* from Apple; or any of several other excellent texts and references.

INITs

When a Mac is started up (also called bootstrapped or just booted), programs resident in the ROM chips are called into action to carry out functions such as self-tests of the various circuits and memory. Once this is done, instructions are issued to try to load a System from a floppy or hard disk. If a System file can be identified, it is loaded from the disk into RAM, the working memory of the computer. The combination of the software found in the ROM and the software contained in the System file loaded from the disk becomes the working System in your machine.

If there is a mistake in the System file or if a new version of a particular routine is made available, Apple releases a new version of the System to allow the altered software to be used. If a change is needed to the software in ROM or to the System, this change must be patched in at system startup time for it to work (remember, the ROM can't be changed; the ROM chips are part of the hardware in the computer). This patching is done at system time through the use of special resources called INITs. They are small pieces of code that the system uses to modify certain software in the loaded System. INITs don't modify the System stored on disk or in ROM; they just affect the working System. INITs can also be used to change the way in which the System handles certain functions; for example:

- An INIT can place a picture on your Mac screen and cause it to remain on the screen all the time your Mac is powered on (your working windows appear on top of the picture);
- INITs are available as packages like *EasyAccess* and *CloseView* that assist the physical or visually handicapped user (available at no charge from Apple and included in new System releases starting with System Version 6.0);
- INITs can allow almost unlimited numbers of fonts and/or Desk Accessories in your System (bypassing Apple's limit of 15 DAs);
- An INIT can be used as a patch that will make a log entry into a file every time your Mac is booted up; and
- INITs can be patches supplied with various after market hardware components (hard disk drives, large screens, printers, scanners, and such) to patch the System and allow these devices to work with the Mac.[11]

INITs are available commercially or as shareware or freeware. At last count, we identified over 250 available INITs. Why are there so many? Since INITs are

---

[11]DOS machines have similar after-market programs such as printer drivers and mouse drivers.

essentially little sub-programs designed to work with a System, programmers use them to develop new features on the Mac. (Recall all those resources and the overall modular concept of the Mac. INITs can be virus programs too.)

Implementing an INIT is easy. With System 4.0 or later,[12] you simply copy the INIT into the System Folder and reboot the Mac. When the System is loaded, all INITs found in the System Folder are executed. An INIT is simply executable code, and it can do just about anything it wants to when it runs--including things like modifying applications, inserting code or other resources into files, and deleting resources such as data. Does this sound a lot like a computer virus?

Because INITs attempt to modify a rather complicated program (the actual System), they themselves are often rather complicated little pieces of code. Sometimes they're not tested as thoroughly as they should be. For example, one of us received an INIT that was supposed to preserve the contents of the Clipboard over a System crash. After testing, he installed it on a production system, and it seemed to work fine. Then one day there was a crash while a large amount of data was in the Clipboard; when he tried to reboot, all he got was the infamous MacBomb--and the system would no longer boot. After some hours of diagnosis, the problem was traced to the way the INIT worked.

Was this a virus? Probably not. More likely, the programmer thought he or she had developed a truly useful tool but simply didn't test it thoroughly enough. But it could have been a virus or Trojan Horse.

How do you protect yourself from intentionally damaging unproven INITs? Basically, you can use the same methods as for any other new piece of software. Test it thoroughly on a secure locked system before allowing it onto your production machine. Make backups of your materials before you implement new INITs. The precautions are similar for any system, and are covered in more detail in Chapter 7.

A couple of warnings are needed here. Because INITs are patches to the system, they can be rather tricky little pieces of programming and often do things that well-behaved programs shouldn't do. Many virus protection packages will interpret these actions as potential virus activity.[13] What do you do to determine whether your suspect INIT is a virus or just some fancy programming?

Try .i.testing; it; rely on the source (commercial.i. INIT;s are less likely to harbor disease, just as commercial software is less likely to be infected); don't use it (if you got it from a BBS and can't check its origin is it worth the risk?); or

---

[12]To see what system version you have, choose About the Finder . . . when you are on the DeskTop (Release 4.1 or later).

[13]We won't go into this in detail, since to tell whether the unusual activity is okay or the result of a virus you need some detailed technical knowledge. This is true on DOS machines as well.

examine it with *ResEdit* or a virus protection tool. If you feel you lack sufficient skill with such tools, you might contact the nearest Mac Users' Group. Your local dealer may be able to help you find such a group.

cdevs

Macintosh systems offer a Desk Accessory called the Control Panel.[14] It allows you to control a number of the attributes of your Mac and configure it to match your work habits and method of doing things more closely. Early versions of the Control Panel were fixed and you could only change the functions it contained: DeskTop pattern, insertion pointer blink rate, sound volume level, mouse tracking speed, and such. Later versions were redesigned so that you can add resources to the Control Panel that you wish to change. These are added by entities called cdevs (control panel devices). In many ways cdevs are similar to INITs, but cdevs have an additional feature: They're available after the System is up and running and may be modified any time. Everything that has been said about INITs applies to cdevs; cdevs also may be obtained commercially or from BBSs.

Apple has converted all the functions that the Control Panel can modify into cdevs. These include Mouse (controls the actions of the mouse), General (most attributes of the Mac), and Keyboard (functions of the keyboard such as repeat rate, and the alphabet used and how it relates to keys). Some after-market cdevs are:

- A modification to the Sound Manager that lets you tell the Mac to play back one of several sounds instead of simply beeping to indicate an error (e.g., organ music, "glass breaking," HAL saying "I'm sorry Dave, but I'm afraid I can't do that.");

- For color monitors, a cdev that lets you change the color attributes of various parts of windows and menus;

- *Vaccine*, a cdev that functions as a protector by stopping the computer and informing the operator if a program tries to modify System resources; and

- *GuardDog*, a security cdev that makes it harder for a casual user to copy, rename, or delete files from the system (this also has an interesting sound effect).

The last two are reviewed in the Appendix.

---

[14]Some packages on DOS machines, like *Windows*, *GEM*, and the *Presentation Manager*, offer similar capabilities.

BULLETIN BOARDS

In the microcomputer world, bulletin boards are simply programs running on the system. A BBS operator will have one or more hard disks, and will set up partitions to keep things in their proper compartments. The bulletin board can serve as a medium for infection, by having diseased programs available to be downloaded by users. Such programs won't affect the BBS unless they are run by the BBS operator. BBS operators need to be very careful about running programs when they're not sure of the source, especially since they may deal with dozens or hundreds of people.

Since the BBS operator probably uses one of a small number of available, good BBS programs, and since he or she is a visible target, the exposure is greater. Also, the skill level of the vandal may be higher; it's more "satisfying" to corrupt something big; that way, you get newspaper headlines. If you operate a BBS, you'd be well advised to have several antiviral programs, and to be rather stringent about practicing safe hex.

Remember too that although it is very difficult to break into your bulletin board from normal communications channels, back doors may be available. In Chapter 2, we looked at some of the standard penetration methods.[15] Many of these may apply not to your BBS but to the operating system of the computer that runs the BBS. This whole area quickly gets into security implications that don't differ much from any other minicomputer or mainframe operation (we don't cover them here). Be aware that if your BBS is on a mini or a mainframe you could get caught by someone coming in through a back door, and take precautions.

EXPOSURES

Remember that someone has to *put* a virus into your system. The most common way for that to happen is by means of a Trojan Horse program.[16] You like a program; you download and run it; the included virus does its nasty thing. The person who put the virus onto your system is you. (We have met the enemy and they are us?)

---

[15]Trojan Horses, Salamis and Other Computer Delights

[16]There are other possibilities, including intercepting communication lines. Ask yourself again, "Does anyone dislike *me personally* that much?"

Freeware and Shareware

Freeware refers to programs that are in the public domain, available for you to download at your leisure. If there's a charge or registration fee, it's shareware. This is one of the profoundly exciting things about connectivity: Millions of people can share with each other, and everyone wins. Since there are thousands of freeware and shareware programs, you can't expect a BBS operator to test every one. Some of the most popular ways to get a virus into your system are, therefore, through these programs. This is not an exhaustive list, but you'd be advised to be careful if you decide to accept these exposures.

Disk/Diskette Compression Utilities

Disk and diskette compression utilities are very popular and useful. Since they normally access things like FAT areas during their operation, they're also wonderful places to put a virus. Be careful; several viruses have been transmitted by using such programs. A similar exposure is to the ARC and un-ARC programs used to compress and decompress data for transfer between your system and a BBS. They're common because compressed programs take less storage and less transmission time. If the compression program is infected, it can infect anything you compress or expand.

Fake Games (e.g., SEX.EXE)

Games have been notorious for spreading diseased software. Typically, people download a new game (and new ones appear all the time), then run it immediately. Since you're concentrating on the game, you might not notice that it's doing other things as well. Who can resist running a program named SEX? That particular program happens to spread a virus that messes around with FAT areas. Again, don't be turned off totally, but do be very careful.

Pirate Copies

Your friend gives you a copy of a program he or she stole. By accepting it you are dealing in stolen goods. Do you trust your friend? Do you know where he or she got the program? We recommend that you support software developers by paying for your programs. It's much safer.

Updates for Software Distributed by Networks

Another potential for a valuable-looking Trojan Horse is upgrades and fixes for programs distributed by software developers. Many of the larger developers distribute programs and upgrades on public domain BBSs. Your problem as a user is to be sure that no one modified the upgrade to include a disease once it was outside the developer's control. Some of the antiviral programs (see the Appendix) have the ability to scan a file for known viruses. We recommend you use them before running *anything* from a BBS, whether it's freeware, shareware, or a program upgrade. Or you could simply get the upgrade directly from the developer, although that takes more time for mailing and such.

Communication Channels

Any time you communicate with another computer, you use some channel. It may be a wire, or more likely a telephone call. Although we do not deal with communications exposures, be aware that phone lines can be tapped. You might not be talking only to the computer you think you are. If you think you're exposed to this kind of sophisticated vandalism, get a book on the subject and develop your own expertise, or hire professionals.

HOW TO CREATE VACCINES, REMEDIES

This chapter discussed how computer viruses reproduce themselves and gave some common things they do. This section is for vaccine developers, who should look to creating tools that examine virus exposures. We encourage you to work on vaccines: Most people don't have much of a chance without such help.

There are three basic needs in virus protection:

- Detect;
- Prevent; and
- Repair damage.

A vaccine should be able to recognize diseased software; this helps people avoid viruses in the first place. It can scan files for known viruses and enable users to look for suspicious text in program files (such as the apocryphal HA HA GOTCHA). Naturally, a new virus won't be found this way, unless the vandal is kind enough to include funny messages in the code in a readable format. A method that helps limit the damage is to make sure that programs affected by viruses are discovered. This can be done by using some form of signature, encryption, or combinations. A vaccine might also search for TSR calls and low-level disk or memory access commands in the code. Be sure you provide good documentation so users can distinguish between a virus and when a program does this sort of thing on purpose.

Since you can't scan for viruses you don't know about, the next level of protection is to try to trap the common nasty things these diseases do, so as to limit the damage. The vaccine might include a memory resident program that traps system calls, TSR calls, attempts to format a disk, or attempts to modify a program or system file.[17]   It might also include an automated or manual signature check so that programs with altered signatures are blocked by the protection program.   Or it can automate an approved program list.   The documentation should make it clear that encryption, signatures, and approval lists don't protect against accidental approval of a diseased program (hence the first item, scanning to screen out garbageware in the first place). Some means of locking out access to files might be an option (but this gets tricky to implement and is not foolproof).

This sort of damage control can be a selling point: At least one of the protection programs described in the Appendix has added virus control to existing capabilities and the developer reports increased sales.

There remains the problem of developing a wide spectrum antiviral agent that will protect against all virus attacks, both from known and from presently unknown viruses. To date, such an application does not exist. One reason is that for a virus to do its dirty work, it accesses the system and issues the same type of requests that a legitimate program might use.[18] How is the antiviral agent to differentiate between a proper application requesting a function of the operating system to perform a legitimate and desired task and a virus making the same request? From the point of view of the antiviral agent, one looks pretty much like the other.   The analogy often drawn between cancer in humans and virus programs in computers is appropriate here.

The final component of a protection system is some means of repairing damage. Saving various data such as CMOS, boot sectors, and FAT copy helps in recovery from some problems.   Utilities such as *ResEdit* (Macintosh), *PCTOOLS*, *Norton Utilities*, and *Mace Utilities* (DOS) are the likely solutions. This is outside the scope of a strictly virus-protection scheme, but the documentation could give some pointers here.   The documentation shouldn't be too detailed; people who don't know the details of DOS or Macintosh shouldn't be using tools like this in the first place. Mention that in your documentation as well.

---

[17]As a developer, you presumably are a sophisticated programmer as well. You should get copies of the technical material not in this book; the References will help. You should be aware of the research efforts trying to determine the ways viruses attach to programs, and the 40 or so most common things viruses do to systems. Dr. Highland's forthcoming book may be your ticket. The journal *Computers & Security* is an excellent source.

[18]Dr. Highland has reported some progress in identifying a small number of characteristics shared by all viruses on DOS systems. If his research can prove such a short list, a general virus protection system need only find ways to block all of them. It would apply to new as well as known viruses. Some argue that such a list is not possible.

Don't forget the risk of a virus targeting the protection program. Strategies such as user-chosen pathnames and filenames for authorization tables, encryption of tables, and signatures for protection programs have been published.[19]

---

[19]For example, [Madsen 1988]

Chapter 6

HACKERS, PIRACY, VIRUSES, AND YOUR MONEY

Some things people do sure make my life easy. Everyone passes around games. If I can infect a game-passer, he or she probably copies other programs too and I can get at those programs as well. Wow! There sure are a lot of people doing that.

HACKERS

Many studies of personality and motivations for criminal behavior have been done. The vandal who uses computer virus programs to do damage is in some ways not very different from any other criminal, and in some ways quite different.

People have different personalities. It's been reported[1] that of a large group of people, perhaps 85 percent are basically honest, 5 percent would try something if they thought there was little or no chance of being caught, another 5 percent would risk even a fifty-fifty chance, and 5 percent would try something even if it's nearly certain that they'll be caught (we'd call this last group psychopaths or sociopaths) (Figure 6.1). There are enough people who have the skills needed to create a virus that these percentages likely apply: That is, we need to be concerned about the 10 percent or so who will risk high odds of being caught.

People tend to do things for a reason, and the usual motives of profit or revenge apply to people who might create computer virus programs. Some people are simply psychotic, and would spread a software disease as an act of senseless vandalism. Other people do it for intellectual challenge. The best computer professionals may be tempted to respond to a challenge like "my system is unbreakable."

---

[1][Krauss 1979] especially Chapter 2

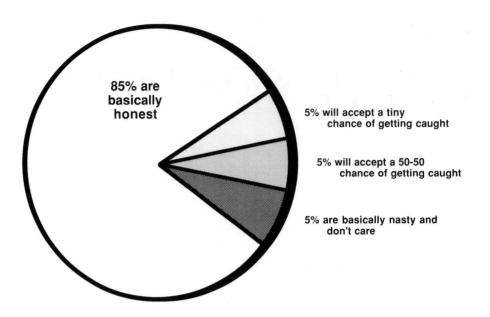

Figure 6.1 Types of People

A joy in intellectual challenges is one of the things that makes a good professional; but a challenge like the one above is a also a red flag to a hacker.[2]

Protection from criminals involves elements of personality, opportunity, and motives. As a computer user, you can limit the hacker's opportunity by practicing safe hex. As an employer, you can affect the motivation by providing good working conditions and pay scales. As an ethical human being, you can avoid practices like spreading viruses. If you must enter the fray, it's much more challenging to devise protection schemes, and more socially acceptable, than to crack systems.

---

[2]See [Landreth 1987] for a really scary discussion of the motives of some hackers. They don't care about the odds or potential damage; all they have is a need to respond to the technical challenge and have people appreciate their "genius." One way to catch them, in fact, is to appeal to their vanity while keeping them on the phone long enough for a trace.

WITH A LITTLE HELP FROM MY FRIENDS: PIRACY

There are one or two things that you should consider if you're thinking of creating and spreading a virus. First, in addition to it being despicable and unprofessional behavior, it's against the law.

Most viruses spread through various violations of copyright laws or licenses. When you "buy" a program, in most cases you don't actually own the program, just the right to use it under certain conditions. The conditions typically include not passing around free copies, that is, not pirating copies.

Some of the things that happen when you spread a virus are covered under criminal law. The exact laws vary from place to place, but the point is you can get into serious trouble if you're caught.[3] (And if you're not caught, who will know how bright you were?) Chapters 10 and 11 deal with legal aspects of computer virus programs.

Piracy also is one of the most common transmission vectors for computer viruses. Are you sure who the donor is? Is the BBS secure and sterile? Where did your friend get it? You should ask yourself these questions. How careful should you be about the source of your programs? Computer programs are the lifeblood of your computer. How careful would you be about the source if you required a blood transfusion?

Figure 6.2, for example, shows a 1986 poster prepared by the United States National Computer Security Center. Notice how they take the virus threat *very* seriously. Think about it. You should take it seriously too.

---

[3]You may spend time in prison, be faced with fines, and carry a criminal record that can ruin your life.

Figure 6.2 "Never Accept Gifts from a Stranger"

TANSTAAFL: WHY THAT PACKAGE COSTS $1000

TANSTAAFL is a word we first saw in a book by Robert A. Heinlein, *The Moon is a Harsh Mistress*. It's made up from the initials of the words "There Ain't No Such Thing As A Free Lunch." The basic principle is that nothing is free: Someone, somewhere, pays the cost of whatever the gift is. You may see that program your friend offers you as free. But there's a cost. Widespread piracy is one of the reasons the good programs can cost a lot of money, as well as one of the most common transmission paths for spreading viruses.

Computer programs don't grow on trees; people have to create them. Writing good programs is not easy, and it's not cheap. To get an idea why, take a look at Figure 6.3, which depicts some of the major tasks in the process of developing and marketing a good program, the kind that you will buy and use because it makes your life easier.[4] Let's look at each step briefly, keeping in mind that this list is oversimplified; if you want more technical detail, see a reference on systems analysis.

• Problem Definition

Problem Definition is a critical step. If the problem hasn't been defined, it can't be solved. One thing professionals have learned is that mistakes at this stage are *very* expensive to clean up later. For application software, if developers spend a lot of money developing a wonderful solution that has to search for a problem, they're likely lose their shirts. This step doesn't have to cost a great deal, but it's critical.

• Design and Development

Design and Development is where the programs are actually written. It's not usually the most expensive step, but that doesn't mean it's easy or cheap. Programs such as *Lotus 1-2-3*, *dBase 3*, or Microsoft *Word* take many person years to develop. Depending on the complexity of the programs, there's probably an investment of from $100,000 to millions of dollars in this stage. Keep in mind that a virus can infect a program during this process.

---

[4]Depending on the marketing and other strategies of the developer, many of these costs are highly variable. Different marketing strategies, for example, can double the cost of a program. Although the relative costs will differ, all the activities have to happen for good programs to be created.

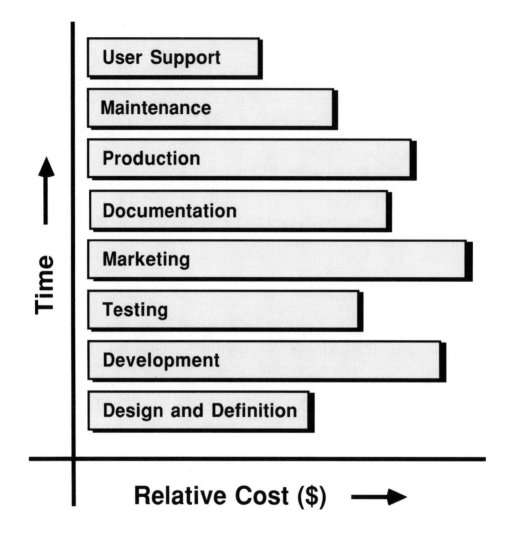

Figure 6.3 Relative Costs of Software Development

• Testing

Another good way to go broke is to release a buggy program, one with lots of errors. To avoid this, many things have to be done, but testing is one crucial step. Developer have to test things as well as possible. They need to do a beta test, where copies of the program are released to a group of testers not closely connected with the company. Depend on it: They'll find problems the company people missed.[5] Fix these problems, and there won't be as many unhappy customers. Unhappy customers cost sales and time to fix bugs. This is also a good time to be sure there aren't any viruses or logic bombs hiding anywhere.

• Marketing

At some point, people have to be convinced to buy the program. There are, very roughly, four ways to sell an application program:

- Wear out shoes trying to sell it to individuals and dealers;
- Distribute it as shareware and hope enough people like it and send money that there's a profit;
- Build up a market slowly through limited advertising, referrals, and such; and
- Spend *a lot* of money on advertising to sell many copies of the program very quickly.

We'll look at this more deeply below: Piracy and viruses affect marketing strategy and thus costs.

• Documentation

Ideally, every program should be completely self-documenting, with terrific help screens, easy-to-use logical functions, and so on. Real world programs that do complex things aren't ideal. Developers must create good manuals. They must show people what the program does, list errors and what to do about them, and other things. Good documentation is hard to write and expensive to create and to produce, but it's necessary.

• Production

---

[5]This isn't a dig at developers; there are sound psychological reasons why programmers should never be the only ones to test their own work. It's a good idea to have a group of formal testers and not to sell beta versions. You make customers unhappy that way and get a bad reputation.

Production is the time to produce lots of copies of documentation and program diskettes. Copying can be done by the developer, or by companies that specialize in it. In any case, the masters go somewhere, they're copied, some kind of quality control is applied, they're packaged with the manuals and shrink-wrapped. There are quite a few places in this process where a virus can creep into a master. It's happened.

•Maintenance/Upgrades

If developers want to be around for long, there has to be a process for fixing reported bugs in programs, and distributing fixes and upgrades to customers. It's crucial to be sure that the fixes and upgrades aren't diseased. As a cost item, research and development can be put in this category.

•User Support

Last on our list, and on some developers' lists, is user support. People likely will buy more from a company that offers a service to help them use the software. If there are many customers, this can get to be an expensive proposition, and in any case it involves a long-term commitment.

Let's get back to the marketing effort in more detail, and look at the effects of viruses and piracy. Remember that if the developer doesn't sell enough programs, there won't be a profit, and if the developers don't make a profit they won't be around long.

Now look at what piracy does to this process. Piracy means there will be a lot of freebies out there for every one of the programs that are paid for. Estimates range from 2 to 30 or more pirate copies for every legitimate copy, over the lifetime of the program.[6] If a program is good, people will want to copy it, and as time goes on there will be more pirate copies. What does this do to profits? And to the chance of the developer staying in business?

One effect of piracy is to force a developer to use one of two marketing strategies: Distribute as shareware (low cost but high risk, and lots of exposure to virus infection), or set up a huge marketing campaign (*very* expensive). Both work, but in different ways and for specific types of software. The shareware approach is suitable for software that appeals to a mass market. Since most software fits niche markets, the return from a shareware approach is so dismal it isn't feasible.

Now back to TANSTAAFL. A major reason software is so expensive is that *someone* has to pay for that very expensive advertising. If a developer has a hot

---

[6]The experience of the *MacMag* virus, which hit 350,000 machines in two months, suggests that these estimates may be wildly low.

number, enough copies to make a decent profit must be sold *fast*. Soon enough the demand will be met by pirate copies, and there's no return from those. That kind of advertising blitz can cost millions, sometimes more than all the other costs together.

The need to use an expensive advertising campaign forced by rampant piracy has all sorts of other implications. Proper testing, especially beta testing, takes time. If a developer has committed big bucks to an advertising campaign with a release date, the programmers are under enormous pressure to produce on time. That kind of pressure leads to mistakes, one kind being inadequate control that may allow viruses into the software. Bugs and poor documentation due to deadline pressure are other common problems.

Another pressure is brought on by things like discovering bugs a week before the scheduled release date. There's a huge temptation to release a buggy version rather than to hold back for further testing. This is where vaporware comes from. That's acceptable if unfortunate: At least the motive is good, to avoid releasing programs with errors in them.

Some developers, hardware and software alike, have been accused of using vaporware as a marketing strategy. This technique does not make fans among the users or hopeful users of the software or hardware.

Notice that piracy has been a major cause of a lot of problems,[7] including buggy programs and vaporware, and, of course, much higher costs just to pay for all those ads. Now add viruses into that picture. What all this implies is that reliable software is about to get even more expensive. The only way for a developer to deal with viruses is to enforce tighter controls and more testing in several phases of the development process. That adds costs and takes time.

In conclusion, piracy and viruses together look likely to account for more than half the cost of most good and reliable programs, and also to delay availability. There just may not be as many good programs coming out, even for pirates to copy.

---

[7]It's estimated [Wyles 1988] that corporate piracy is responsible for a stunted software industry in Italy. We're not talking about small effects here.

Chapter 7

HOW CAN I AVOID VIRUSES: SAFE HEX

Let's see, what shall I do next? Let's look over there . . . oh, oh, what's that program already in there up to? Is that a vaccine? Am I in danger? Rats, I can't get in, and that program is trying to write to my

Three things are involved in coping with viruses:

1. Avoiding them in the first place;
2. Discovering them and getting rid of them; and
3. Repairing the damage.

Chapters 8 and 9 deal with diagnosing and curing systems infected with computer viruses. Here, we look at things you can do, and things you should avoid doing, so you can keep viruses out of your system in the first place. This ounce of prevention could save you a lot of time in applying pounds of cure.

THINGS TO DO, AND THINGS TO LEAVE UNDONE

DO: To be safest, purchase all your programs, shrink-wrapped, from a reputable dealer.

This isn't realistic all the time, of course. And also remember that a dealer could break the shrink wrap and re-wrap the program. Moreover, original shrink-wrapped software can already be infected. One of us has purchased original shrink-wrapped software, only to find that the internal "break this seal" envelope containing the disks was already open.

DO: Every time you get a new program:

- Write-protect a master (or original) diskette before inserting it into a drive;[1] and

- If you download shareware to a hard disk, copy it onto a data diskette (*not* a system disk) and delete it from your hard disk *before running the program*; then write-protect the diskette to improve your odds.

You now have an original, non-bootable diskette for testing purposes. There's no system on the diskette to get infected if the program is diseased. Also, since you did not run a downloaded program from your hard disk, your hard disk is still safe.

DO: Make a backup copy, using the original write-protected diskette as the input. Write-protect the backup copy you've made too; that improves your odds. (If your system is already infected the backup copy may be infected as you create it.)

DO: Install the program from the write-protected *original* diskette (or first copy you made if you downloaded shareware to your hard disk).

You're working with your original, or first, copy; it's the least likely to be infected and you've minimized any chance of further infection by write-protecting the diskette. (There is a small risk that any backup copy you've made is itself contaminated.)

DO: Compare the files from the original or first diskette with the same files on your backup copy. If there's any difference at all, you can suspect a virus. (Use DISKCOMP or COMP on a DOS machine, or any other compare utility you're comfortable with.)

DO NOT: Continue if you find differences. Your system is probably infected;[2] go to Chapter 8 to confirm this or to Chapter 9 for advice on disinfecting your system.

---

[1]You might need that original to recover from any number of problems, and write-protection is the best insurance you can get.

[2]Some programs modify themselves, for instance, to save information such as your user name and password. These will test different to the compare although there's nothing wrong. We hope the manufacturers will change this habit; there's no way for the average user to tell whether there's a questionable programming practice or a virus infection. *Think*, developers: There's a *reason* the ALTER verb was dropped from COBOL.

DO: Test any new program you have. Does it do what you want? Does it act funny? Do you see any of the virus symptoms described in Chapter 8? (If possible, run this test on a separate computer with no hard disk, no CMOS, and no communication capability.)

If the program is shareware and it doesn't work, get rid of it. If there are virus symptoms, you may have infected your system, but most likely the virus is in "copy myself" mode and hasn't done anything else--yet. Therefore, you still may have a chance to use some of the less drastic methods in Chapter 9 to disinfect your system, and avoid discovering what the virus might have done after it decided enough copies were made.

DO: If you want extra safety from viruses, try this: Re-run all of your tests with the system clock set for a date one month later; with a date one year later; and with some Friday the 13th (use the TIME and DATE commands in DOS, or reset the clock from the Control Panel on a Macintosh). (Remember to reset your timer to the correct date and time after you're finished.)

If the virus contains a time bomb, you'll likely set it off with one or more of these clock changes, and the test results will change. (If you're worried about political viruses like the PLO virus, try politically significant dates as well as Friday the 13th.) If the test results differ, you're infected; go to Chapter 9.

DO: Check new programs for suspicious text strings. If you find any, destroy the program (and the diskette, to be absolutely safe; this is a lot cheaper than fixing any lingering damage if you use an infected diskette later by mistake).

Open the program as a data file with a word processor or editor. If possible, open it in read-only mode. Scan through the program looking for things like Gotcha! or Dummy! Most of the program will look like junk; you may see some readable error messages, copyright notices, menu choices, and such. Insulting or "cute" messages are common in virus code.[3] Don't change the program in any way (if it's on a write-protected diskette you probably can't), and don't save it from your editor or word processor. You're just looking, and unless you really know what you're doing you can't make *any* change to a program with an editor or word processor that won't ruin the program.

DO: If you have any antiviral programs, scan the program for known viruses.

---

[3]In a game or similar program, you might reasonably expect to find such messages, and this method of looking for possible viruses won't be much help to you.

DO: On a DOS computer take a look at any .BAT files and at your CONFIG.SYS file regularly, perhaps monthly, and also every time you load or test a new program.

Since a virus has to be run to make copies or do damage, it sometimes will insert lines into an AUTOEXEC.BAT or CONFIG.SYS file. If you find new lines, or changes to ones you already have, suspect a virus and go to Chapter 8 or 9.

DO: If you have special utilities such as we've mentioned, look for hidden files (DOS) or invisible files (Macintosh).

Some legitimate programs use hidden or invisible files, but they're also a favorite place for a virus to hide things. If you find any (besides normal system files), take care.[4]

DO: If your system does not have a hard disk, always boot from a write-protected diskette.

If the system on your boot disk is write-protected (by using the physical protect tab), it's extremely unlikely that any virus will infect those system files.

DO: Record file lengths, creation date, and creation time on critical backups.

Log this information somewhere; if you ever need to restore from a backup you'll be able to check to see that nothing obvious has changed.

DO: If you have a program that will do some kind of checksum, run it and record the results. Frequently, perhaps even every time you run a program, re-run the checksum and compare against your record to be sure it hasn't changed.

Many of the antiviral packages include some form of checksum. It lets you be pretty sure you're restoring from the original and not from an infected copy. There's no protection if the original is infected, of course. It'll stay unchanged and still infected.

DO: Keep logs of every new program you put into your system. Record the length, date and time, checksum if you have one, and when and where you got the program. Record the dates and such for any backup copies you have.

If you ever do discover a virus, you'll bless these logs; they allow you to go back to find out what program was loaded just before the virus showed up,

---

[4]Check Chapter 5 for some normal hidden and invisible files. Some of the antiviral agents include this sort of scan capability; see the Appendix.

to find backups that date before the infection, and so on. You may be able to go after the vandal if you can find out who gave you the program and when.

DO: Avoid obvious risks. Download only from sources you trust, accept programs only from people you know and trust, and so on. The idea is to avoid getting diseased software. Developers, ethical professionals, ethical BBSs, and so on, don't knowingly deal in diseased software.

VACCINES

Several of the products discussed in the Appendix have capabilities we've been mentioning, like checksums, automated approved-program lists, and known-virus scans. You can improve your odds against a virus infection by using one or more of these products, especially the kind that keeps a list of approved programs and complains if you try to run an unapproved program, or one that has changed since you approved it. (This does *not* protect you if you authorized an already-infected program; be sure it's clean before you authorize it.)

DO: If you think you are in a high-risk group, buy and install one of the antiviral packages that lets you scan new programs for known viruses and traps unapproved programs or approved programs that try to do unexpected and sensitive things.

Note that virus protection programs must work on the same parts of your system that commonly are targeted by viruses. If there's a bug in the protection program, it can do pretty much the same things that a virus could do. This point relates to our cautions about using special utilities in recovering from virus attacks; these utilities also allow you to alter sensitive parts of your operating system.

A vaccine that scans for known viruses has one obvious problem: It won't find new or unknown ones. This is part of the reason we continue to emphasize that *nothing* gives perfect protection. Developers of vaccines that scan for viruses normally send out updates as they find new viruses. Often, they also ask you to send them any viruses you find, so that any new ones can be added to the vaccine program. Do it; you'll help a lot of people avoid the problem you just had.

MORE ABOUT BACKUPS

We may be getting a bit tedious about backups. But the reason is a good one: Through repetition you'll get the idea that we consider backups *important*. In fact, they're *crucial*.

DO: Make backups.

If you don't have backups, anything that goes wrong can really mess you up. You can't just restore from before the problem; you have to start over. Remember, even if viruses are not very likely, power failures, program bugs, head crashes, damaged diskettes, and simple mistakes when you get tired *are* common. Most of us need to restore something from a backup every month or two. Usually this is because we goofed and deleted the wrong thing, didn't save something, spilled food or soda on a diskette, or made some similar human error.

> Backups are the single most important action you can take to protect yourself against viral attack. They are also the lowest cost.

DO: Keep more than one backup of important things.

Most viruses will copy themselves to anything they can reach, and that includes the backup diskette. That's partly why you should keep more than one backup (and also *data and program files only* on one set of backup diskettes and system files on a separate set). If you catch a virus, you can then restore your data or programs from an uninfected backup taken before the virus struck. If there are system files on your backup diskettes, a virus is likely to corrupt them and you'll re-infect your computer when you try to restore from the backup.

If you have the right virus-protection programs, there are some very special backups you can, and should, keep. Some of the packages let you make backup copies of your boot sectors, FAT tracks, and maybe even the data in CMOS. These can be invaluable if you ever have to fix virus damage. You may be able to recover from a hard disk problem simply by restoring the boot sector and/or FAT track, which is a whole lot easier than rebuilding your hard disk from scratch.

DO: Label backups with date and time created. Log other pertinent data.

If you're a company, you might consider using one of the standard rotation schemes in your backups. See, for example, any introductory text in computers for a description of the grandfather, father, son method.

DO: Keep backups for a while; you might have to go back a ways to find an uninfected one if you're trying to recover from diseased software. Six months is not unreasonable.

DO: Write-protect program disks before you install the disks into a drive.

Copy and write-protect the backups. Using the physical write-protect tabs is your best insurance that a virus can't change anything on the protected disks.

PERSPECTIVE

Remember, you're not too likely to be a target yourself. Perfect safety isn't possible; but you can get a great deal of safety by practicing some common sense rules (safe hex) that cost nothing except a bit of inconvenience. You can also download antiviral programs, some of which offer reasonable protection for shareware prices. Or you can purchase commercial software, some of which is very protective but at a higher cost in dollars and inconvenience. (At some point the added nuisance of the effect of some of these programs on your operation starts to be more annoying than the possibility of a virus.)

Figure 7.1 illustrates something widely known and referred to as the 80/20 rule, or the 90/10 rule. It is simply the principle that you get most of your benefit from the first efforts; that is, the first 20 percent of your money gets you 80 percent of your value, or 20 percent of your products account for 80 percent of your sales, or whatever. Any time you try for perfection, that last little bit gets very expensive.

**90% of the Security
costs 10% of the money**

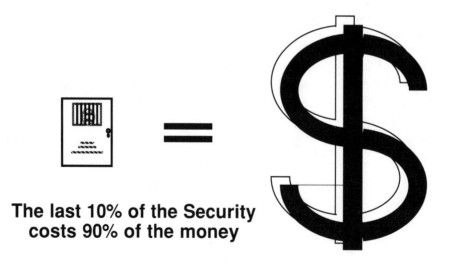

**The last 10% of the Security
costs 90% of the money**

Figure 7.1 90/10 Rule

Chapter 8

IS THAT A "MICRO" ORGANISM?

I can hide pretty well; I look just like some programs, and you can't be sure it's me until it's too late and I've done my nasty thing. Then you'll know: *Kilroy was here!*

Unless you are in one of the high-risk categories noted in Chapter 4, you're not likely to run into a virus. But you *are* likely to run into program bugs. Since a virus is sort of a *deliberate* bug, it can be tricky to tell when you have one or the other.[1] How can you avoid crying wolf?

For most users, there are just two ways to discover a virus:

- Use a virus protection program; or
- You see your computer suddenly do strange things for no reason.

DIAGNOSIS WHILE OPERATING

Some of the virus protection programs involve memory resident activities. These monitor what's going on in your system and will warn you there's a virus around, or at least that a program is trying to do something unexpected and potentially dangerous. If you don't use such programs, here are some signs that can serve as warnings:

---

[1] For the average user, the greatest exposure to problems is, in order: human error; program bugs; power supply problems such as brownouts or static or lightning; and any kind of intentional problem such as a virus. (This order could be different in different circumstances.)

- Available RAM decreases without you loading a memory resident program;
- Your disk drive light comes on when you didn't intend to save anything;[2]
- The system slows down very dramatically;
- The program you are working with suddenly displays an unusual error message;
- DOS displays unexpected error messages, especially INVALID DRIVE SPECIFICATION;
- File sizes change without reason;
- The number of files changes;
- Directory updates take noticeably longer;
- On a Macintosh, the appearance of icons changes for no obvious reason;[3]
- Your keyboard keys suddenly do odd things or don't work at all; or
- The system freezes up or crashes.

You can do some simple checks, which might catch some simple viruses, using normal commands on your system. What you're looking for is changes in sizes of programs, amount of free space left on a diskette, changes in last-modified dates or times, and new files you didn't intend to put there.[4]

On a DOS machine, the DIRectory command will give you a display that looks like this:

```
Volume in Drive A is aaaaa
Directory of A:\
.                        [1]      [2]          [3]
MYFILE   EXE       6666  1-31-87       1:02p
.

nn File(s)      275003 Bytes Free
                          [4]
```

Figure 8.1 DOS DIRectory Output

---

[2]But remember that many programs automatically back up things while working, especially word processors. This is normal even though you may not explicitly have told it to do so.

[3]Some specific symptoms are noted in the descriptions of viruses in Chapter 2.

[4]Many programs use temporary files, and if you abort a run of one of these programs the temporary files may remain. This is not necessarily a virus symptom, but you should delete such files in any case. Some viruses have been reported to hide by using file names mimicking temporary files.

The file size [1] may increase when a virus copies itself into the file. The last modified fields [2] and [3] may change when a virus copies itself into the file. This is especially suspicious if the file is COMMAND.COM, since this file normally changes only when you install an upgraded version of DOS. If a virus copies itself into many files, the disk free space [4] may decrease suddenly and unexpectedly.[5] Although a sophisticated virus can make all of these things look normal, many virus programs aren't that smart. It's worth checking your system once in a while. Remember that this command won't display hidden or system files.

The Macintosh displays files on a disk in a different manner. Since the machine is primarily graphics oriented, the default display is graphical: Files and folders are displayed as icons or small pictures within the window for that file. The top of Figure 8.2 illustrates this default display.

Folders on the Mac are much the same as subdirectories on a DOS machine. They contain other things, files or other folders in the case of the Mac. Like subdirectories in DOS, folders can contain other folders, and so on to any depth needed. It is possible to keep track of several thousand files if you design the structure of your folders or subdirectories carefully.

Several options control how files and folders are displayed. In addition to the display by icon, you may choose a display by name (alphabetical), by date (most recent first), by size (largest first), and so on. The bottom part of Figure 8.2 shows the same folders as the top, this time displayed by date.

If a folder is opened, its contents can be displayed in the same manner. In the top half of Figure 8.3 we have opened the folder VirusBookStuff and displayed the contents in their own window, in this case by name. Individual files have their sizes displayed. To get more information about a file, choose Get Info . . . for the Info window display of name, location, type, size, and date and time of creation and last modification.

Symptoms to look for are the same as for the DOS DIRectory display. Unexpected and unexplained changes in file size or the date last modified may signal virus activity. These displays don't show invisible files or attached resources.

---

[5]The free space also will vary if you are using a program like a print spooler or word processor that keeps a lot of temporary files around.

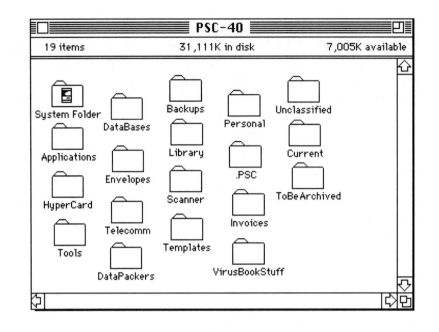

Figure 8.2 Macintosh Directories

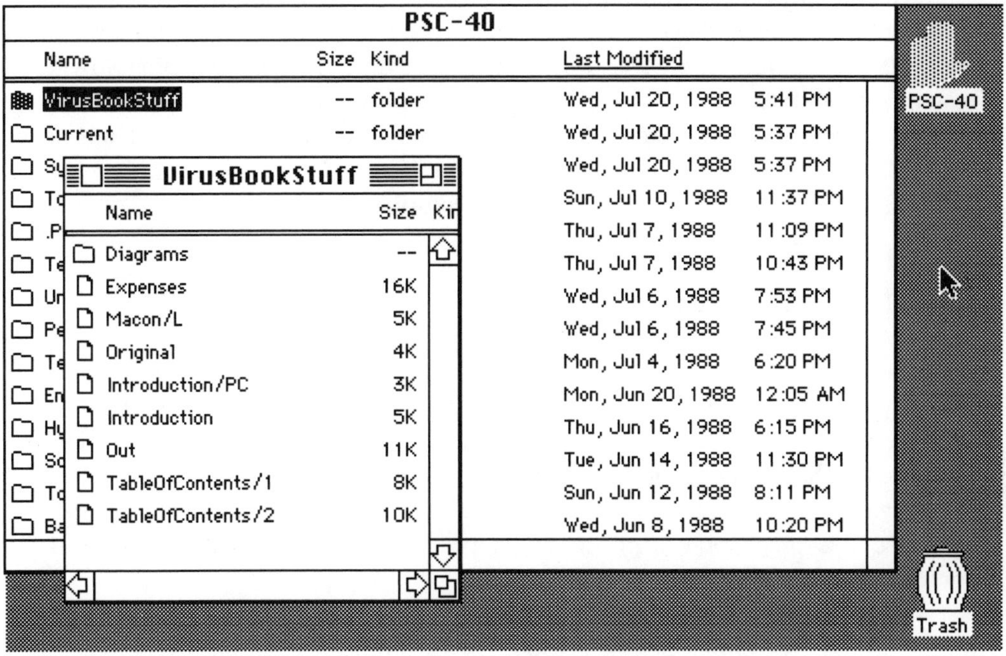

PSC-40

Name	Size	Kind	Last Modified	
VirusBookStuff	--	folder	Wed, Jul 20, 1988	5:41 PM
Current	--	folder	Wed, Jul 20, 1988	5:37 PM
			Wed, Jul 20, 1988	5:37 PM
			Sun, Jul 10, 1988	11:37 PM
			Thu, Jul 7, 1988	11:09 PM
			Thu, Jul 7, 1988	10:43 PM
			Wed, Jul 6, 1988	7:53 PM
			Wed, Jul 6, 1988	7:45 PM
			Mon, Jul 4, 1988	6:20 PM
			Mon, Jun 20, 1988	12:05 AM
			Thu, Jun 16, 1988	6:15 PM
			Tue, Jun 14, 1988	11:30 PM
			Sun, Jun 12, 1988	8:11 PM
			Wed, Jun 8, 1988	10:20 PM

VirusBookStuff

Name	Size	Kin
Diagrams	--	
Expenses	16K	
Macon/L	5K	
Original	4K	
Introduction/PC	3K	
Introduction	5K	
Out	11K	
TableOfContents/1	8K	
TableOfContents/2	10K	

Info

VirusBookStuff
Kind: folder
Size: contents total 178,176 bytes

Where: PSC-40, HyperDrive FX

Created: Mon, Jun 6, 1988 9:28 PM
Modified: Wed, Jul 20, 1988 5:43 PM

Figure 8.3 Macintosh Directories II

Of course, any of these things can be caused by you pressing the wrong keys or by program bugs. These symptoms don't necessarily mean that you have a virus. If you do think there's a virus around, however, shut the machine down, restart from a write-protected original diskette, and use antiviral programs to be sure your programs and system files have not been altered. If there are changes, especially in system files, suspect a virus and take steps. If the antiviral agents give a clean bill of health, it's probably just a computer bug.

VIRUSES IN BACKUPS OR DATA FILES

If you're wondering whether there's a virus on a backup diskette, remember first that if your backups weren't in a drive when things became strange, they're probably okay. As a precaution, when making backups, store them as data files, on diskettes that do not contain system files, so they can't be booted and infect the system. On a Macintosh viruses can infect you through executable INITs and cdevs, so this precaution is not as much protection; but on DOS machines it controls exposure fairly well.

On a DOS machine, your data may be messed up (e.g., odd changes that you might mistake for simple spelling errors). This is a nuisance but not likely to be a danger. The only way to check for viruses is to look at the data, either manually or with a virus-protection program.

On a Macintosh, patches to the system can be made via INIT and cdev files. To find out what these files contain, use an antiviral product such as those listed in the Appendix, or a special utility like *ResEdit*. If you really think there's an infection, consult a professional.

In any system, you can take a signature of any file, to tell when it's been changed. This might be done, for example, by adding up the numeric totals of all bytes in the file (letters have a numeric value, too), then dividing by the numeric values of the size plus creation date plus attribute byte or bytes. (Programs that take signatures are available.) If the file changes the signature changes. We don't, however, put too much weight on this as a protection for backups or data files, since you change these files all the time, and re-calculating signatures every time you do so or make a backup would be an enormous nuisance. In our experience, most people won't do it regularly enough to do much good.

VIRUSES IN PROGRAMS

Unlike data files, executable files such as system files, programs, and .BAT files (on DOS machines) normally don't change unless you re-install them. Therefore, recording the length, creation date, and attributes and checking similar information at a later date against this log, will alert you to changes in programs and other files. We recommend this procedure, especially for system files. Some of the virus protection packages noted in the Appendix do this type of check, either for manual comparison or for automated checks before programs get loaded.

As with data files, some of the viral protection products run memory resident and will alert you to possible virus activities, thus cluing you in on the possible presence of a virus.

For maximum safety, never load a program except from an original, write-protected disk from a container on which you personally broke the shrink wrap or other seal. Unless there's a virus in there from the manufacturer, you will be pretty safe. (See also Chapter 7.) This doesn't apply if you download from a BBS; that method is inherently more risky.

As noted in Chapter 7, if you record when you load any new programs you may be able to find out which program was infected and determine which backups and programs could not have been infected (they were clean before the virus and haven't been put into a drive since). This can help you distinguish between bugs and viruses.

YOU CAN NEVER BE COMPLETELY SURE

A virus program can do anything any other program can. In particular, it can (and most do) hide its tracks. One thing a virus can do is to save a copy of the date and attributes, and restore that after the virus finishes copying itself. Some virus programs are very sophisticated and devious about hiding evidence of their presence, until they blow up and trash your data. No procedure will give you perfect protection against viruses, or diagnose their presence without uncertainty. At least, not until they blow up and you can't miss it.[6]

The development of new anti-viral agents and the practice of safe hex promise a brighter future.

---

[6]This statement isn't absolutely true; military systems they claim can't be penetrated by viruses do exist--TCB category A-1, for security specialists--and also if you never communicate or load anyone else's program your risk is as near zero as you could wish.

Chapter 9

I HAVE/HAD ONE:
WHAT DO I DO NOW?

Hey, there's a job well done. That system looks like a battlefield now. Even if that poor victim can clean it up, I've left lots of copies of myself, so I'll just hit him again. Besides, I messed up the FAT pretty good, and I don't think it can be fixed.

Since there are only a few things you can do to get rid of a virus without having technical knowledge, this chapter often recommends that you seek professional advice. But there still are some things you can do: The most important is to make and restore from uninfected backups.

GETTING RID OF A VIRUS

To get rid of a virus, there is really only one thing you can do if you don't have special tools and detailed technical knowledge: Get rid of *everything* the virus *might* have infected and re-create your system from *clean backups*. If you've kept backups, *and they are uninfected*, you'll lose whatever you've done since the backups but you will be operational again. This procedure is rather drastic; it might be less expensive to hire a professional than to throw away and re-create all your work. You'll have to make that decision yourself.

If you haven't kept backups, there isn't much you can do. *Remember: Once a virus has struck, you cannot trust anything the virus could have infected or changed.* That includes any non-write-protected diskette that was in a drive while the virus was around, even before you discovered the virus.

Reloading the System

If your system (COMMAND.COM, IBMDOS.COM, IBMBIO.COM, MSDOS.SYS, IO.SYS) is corrupted, the easy fix is simply to reload the system. (If you're not sure how to reload, get help.) In any case, this fix may make some data on your disk(ette)s unusable. So you may want professional advice.

- Turn off your computer. You can't trust *anything* the virus could have infected. That includes anything running, any data or programs on the hard disk, and any diskette that is in a drive when the virus hits.

- Insert a write-protected backup diskette with the original system on it. Make sure it's *physically* write-protected to minimize the chance that a leftover virus might infect your original system backup diskette. (Changing the files to read-only is *not* enough.)

- Reboot the system as usual. Be sure you boot from the diskette, not the contaminated hard disk.

- Format the hard disk if there is one. Use appropriate parameters so your system will be re-created from the good copy on your write-protected diskette. You'll lose everything on the disk, but you can't trust it anyway. If you have a special utility that actually writes zeros over anything that might have been on the disk, use it.

- Re-build your hard disk from your original, write-protected application program diskettes (the ones the manufacturer provided and that you write-protected and saved). Make sure any .BAT files you created haven't gained any new and interesting commands inserted by a virus.

- If you don't have a hard disk, you'll have to reformat and rebuild all diskettes that have a system on them or haven't been write-protected.

The computer is now restored with clean programs. Next you have to reload your data files. On a DOS system, you are pretty safe with *data* files. They could be damaged and the diskettes could contain copies of viruses, but you won't contaminate things all over again as long as you don't boot from a contaminated disk.

Finding BRAIN-Type Viruses

A BRAIN-type virus could have left itself in hard-to-reach places like CMOS. Some of the antiviral programs can trap many common virus actions, including those from a virus loaded out of CMOS.[1] Once you find there's a virus in CMOS (the vaccine tells you the virus tried to do something and there's no virus anywhere else in any files), you can get rid of it by disconnecting the battery

---

[1]The vaccine program may do other things too; for instance, *NTIVIRUS* freezes your system to let you know that a virus loaded itself into memory that way, thus limiting the damage such a virus could do.

briefly and then reconnecting it and resetting your clock board. We recommend that if you find yourself in this predicament, get professional help unless you're *very* sure you know what you're doing.[2]

If you don't have the technical skills, you really should get professional help. Check the next section for information about the kinds of things your professional needs to know.

WORKING WITH SPECIAL UTILITIES

If you know what you're doing, there are tools that may let you get rid of viruses and clean up some kinds of damage without having to rebuild your hard disk or all your diskettes. Some of the tools you'll need are utilities like *Norton Utilities*, *PCTOOLS*, or *Mace Utilities* (for DOS), or *1st Aid Kit, ResEdit, MacTools*, or *FeditPlus* for Macintosh. You also need to be familiar with things like file systems (HFS and MFS on the Macintosh, for example) and specialized references like *Inside Macintosh* (Addison-Wesley Publishing) or one of the advanced DOS manuals like *Advanced MS-DOS* (Microsoft Press).

> *Caution*: These are very dangerous tools. If you use them wrong you can muck up even better than a virus could. A little knowledge is a dangerous thing: If you have *any doubt at all* as to what to do, don't try using these tools to rebuild a damaged system.

We won't try to give detailed instructions here; if you know what you're up to you don't need them and if you don't you're likely to cause yourself more trouble.

First, use your utilities to find out what happened. Don't run anything else until you're *sure* it's not contaminated. Clean up your system and your programs, then check out your data files. Write-protect files and backup diskettes once you're sure they are clean. You'll have to be certain that all copies of any viruses are destroyed, or you'll simply be re-infected as soon as you start working again.

---

[2]Getting inside your computer to do this involves working with electrical components and sometimes even with a soldering iron. If you don't know electronic repair you could expose yourself to an electrical or fire hazard, or permanently damage your computer. On an AT or PS/2 or Mac you'll have to reload from a CMOS backup before you can restart the machine, which is one very good reason to use a virus protection product that lets you save CMOS information.

We strongly recommend that you obtain one or more antiviral programs and use them as part of your reconstruction, as well as to protect yourself in the future. Some of the virus protection tools scan for known viruses; this will help you to get rid of diseased programs and files. Some of the tools create file signatures so you can discover altered files and limit future virus infection. Some of the tools intercept many things viruses can do to your system, so even if you get infected or re-infected you'll know about it and be able to limit the damage.

USING BACKUPS

Here is a caution for everyone whether or not you have technical skills: *Check the backups before restoring.* Compare the present creation dates, attributes, and lengths against recorded data. DON'T RESTORE IF THEY ARE NOT THE SAME. Remember, however, this isn't complete protection; if your files were already infected when you recorded the size or signature, they will still be infected and the signature or size won't have changed.

About now is when you really need the virus protection programs. You want to avoid re-infecting yourself in the process of restoring your computer to normal operation. Some of the tools, in combination with the specialized utilities mentioned earlier, will let you diagnose and clean up infected backups.

Chapter 10

LEGAL VACCINES

Well, I really messed up their system. I was triggered and corrupted all their data files and programs. Not only that, I made a bunch of copies of myself, so they'll have to deal with my offspring when they try to clean things up. I wonder if any of those things were valuable? I wonder if any of them were irreplaceable?

Oh, I hear the user talking. He says he wants to do something about this. It's an outrage. It might put him out of business. Oh, this is priceless! He wants to sue my creator. Ha! I've heard that before.

With the broad spread of legitimate and unauthorized computer communications and also the rapid and extensive spread of software piracy, the virus has a very fertile ground in which to multiply and spread.

The only limits to what a virus can do are available memory and accessible data files, and the vandal's imagination. (Chapter 3 described some of the more common virus actions reported.) Even if a virus does nothing worse than display a message, it uses scarce resources such as memory and computing power. The effects can range from annoying to devastating.

The computer virus is very much more than a nuisance or a clever prank introduced into a system by a former employee or a third party. Our modern society relies on computer systems and telecommunications as the lifeblood of modern commerce. A number of commentators have used the disease AIDS as an analogy to create some concept of the spread and results of viruses in computer systems. AIDS has had a profound effect on the "sexual revolution" of the 1960s. For advanced societies that are fundamentally reliant on reliable computer and telecommunications systems, the effect of the computer virus phenomenon will have a significant political, economic, and legal impact. Viruses could do to our evolving information sharing what AIDS has done to human sexual relations (Figure 10.1).

Tick... Tick... Tick...

Miss Jane User,
123 Any Street,
Anywhere, Canada

H0H 0H0

A virus is like a letter bomb

Figure 10.1 Letter Bomb

This chapter reviews the phenomenon of computer viruses and looks at some "legal vaccines" that may be available or that may be used to curb or deter the spread of virus phenomena.

TECHNICAL VACCINES

So far, there have been few legal prosecutions of persons installing virus programs in computer systems. Some of the reasons for this are discussed in the next section.

The computer industry, especially in North America, has responded to the computer virus phenomenon in its usual fashion by first seeking a technical solution to the problem. Many software and hardware manufacturers are developing and marketing antiviral programs that detect the presence of a virus in a computer system and then do something to neutralize it. Some technical solutions include disk and memory management capabilities that control things viruses commonly do, as well as control access to the system so a virus won't get in or harm anything significantly if it does.

Another form of technical solution includes procedures to lessen exposure to viruses. For example, an organization might forbid any use of software brought in from outside and any use of pirate copies at all. If such policies can be enforced there's less exposure to infection in the first place. Also, employees won't be able to take clean software home, get it infected on their own systems, and spread the virus into computers at work when they return the software.

Unfortunately, the introduction of computer virus programs finds its roots in fundamentally anti-social and unethical conduct by some people in the computer industry or with sophisticated technical skills (Figure 10.1). Ultimately, as in the case of technical solutions to software piracy (such as many forms of technical copy protection), the technical approach to combatting computer viruses is only part of the solution.[1] Given the potential disruptive effect of computer viruses on the very fundamentals of how society functions,[2] legal measures are needed as well.

LEGAL VACCINES

The solution to the virus problem will have to be much broader than merely specific technical fixes. Since the solution is fundamentally social in nature, the law will be called on to play a role. In this section, we therefore review the types of legal actions that could be brought against a person who introduces a computer virus program into a host program and allows its spread. We discuss various kinds of liability, both criminal and civil, and look at actions that might be brought against BBS operators, software developers, distributors, and retailers for spreading a viral infection.

Law is about responsibilities, rights, and obligations. Criminal law deals with an individual's responsibilities to the state, the governing power. Criminal sanctions apply to conduct of such severity that the weight of the state's power is applied to prosecute the wrongdoer.

Civil law deals with an individual's responsibility to other individuals. This law is based on the relationship between the individuals. Each relationship affecting another person, whether marriage, neighborhood, employment, a sale

---

[1]Something like military escalation is bound to happen with technical solutions to viruses: a competition among vandals and good guys, with the everyone else caught in the cross fire.

[2]Consider the following: A glitch in a telephone computer cost a telephone company a day of long-distance revenue, estimated at the cost of 900,000 calls. Or the potentially disastrous and deadly effect of a virus activating at the wrong time in an air traffic control system, or a chemical process control system.

transaction, or other intentional or thoughtless action, creates rights and obligations.

It is important to remember, however, that the problem is a broad social one and that the law, which ultimately acts after the event, is only one part of the solution. As we'll discuss in Chapter 11, the only effective long-term solution will be the development of more enforceable ethical standards in the computer industry, standards that are fully accepted by the industry and will assist in curbing the problem, combined with technical and procedural solutions and backed up by laws.

Why So Little Action?

The answer to "why so little action" is complex and begins with the virus victim. Many factors affect the victim's ability to bring a legal action. For one thing, the victim rarely knows who the vandal was, and can only determine this identity with the expenditure of considerable money and time. (Once such investigative work is done, however, it seems reasonably clear that the victim would have a basis to bring legal action against the vandal.) For another thing, some victims may not be willing to disclose their vulnerability. Large corporations, especially financial institutions, wish to have their clients view the corporation's computer systems as reliable and secure.[3] *PC Magazine*, in a report of an infection at EDS, a subsidiary of General Motors Corporation, stated that one factor in not releasing information about the virus attack is that, "One of the things we sell a customer is our ability to secure our customers' data, so we're very, very cautious with that."[4] The article went on to quote from an interview with Dr. Harold Highland, editor-in-chief of *Computers and Security* magazine, where he says, "My recommendation to a corporate entity would be to deny it immediately. I have advised industry that if anything like this happens and you can kill it by denying it, kill it."

The victim of the virus attack will find the primary barrier in suing the vandal is the investigative hurdle of establishing the ultimate source of the virus. The victim, however, does have a direct relationship with the person from whom he or she acquired the diseased software. In the case of commercial acquisition or licensing of software from a reputable dealer, the victim may seek compensation from the dealer or retailer for the injury done. In at least one reported incident, a dealer was notified by customers that they had received infected software, and the dealer took action to ensure that their remaining stock was not infected,

---

[3][Seymour 1988] This is covered in more detail in Chapters 1 and 2.

[4]This has been reported in several industry sources, for example [Cortino 1988].

including erasing hard disks on machines that could have been exposed. Basically, the victim's argument is that the computer dealer or retailer has a duty of care to take reasonable measures to ensure that software sold or licensed to the user/victim will not be infected by viruses. Moreover, reports of the infection of Aldus Corporation's *Freehand* software package with the *MacMag* virus prior to commercial release should cause some concern both to developers and to retailers or dealers of software packages.

Software developers and retailers or dealers have responsibilities to exercise reasonable care to prevent virus contamination. Although there is no definition of reasonable care in this matter and no precautions will guarantee 100% protection, methods recommended in this book are presently expected to be effective and may be factors considered by a court in determining what constitutes reasonable care. Note that what is reasonable varies depending on who is under consideration; a dealer could not reasonably examine shrink-wrapped software for possible virus contamination, for instance. But the dealer or retailer could allow the user/customer to run newly acquired software on a clean machine and scan the software with several antiviral software products. This may be a new area of business for dealers or retailers. They must, however, take reasonable steps to keep such a virus testing clinic free of computer viral infection.

The duty and potential liability of software developers, distributors, retailers and dealers does not indicate that responsibility has shifted from the vandal to these innocent third parties. Rather, because these parties deal in computer software for commercial gain and are, or should be, aware of the computer virus problem, they have an additional duty to the user/customer to take reasonable steps to preclude virus contamination. Given the increasing technical sophistication of new computer viruses, liability will be determined on a case-by-case basis. For example, these innocent third parties may not be liable for a virus that escapes reasonable testing; it is not technically feasible to detect all virus contamination.[5]

Naturally, the developers, distributors, and retailers would seem to have a basis for successful legal action against the vandal who introduced a particular virus into their system with resulting damage, inconvenience, and costs. In the Aldus Corporation case noted earlier, the corporation is reported to have contacted registered users and recalled infected software; the costs of this action and the damage to the reputation of the developer are examples of types of damage that might be claimed against the vandal.

---

[5]In particular, one may scan for *known* viruses, but since new forms and means of virus attack are unknown it is not possible to scan for potential unknown viruses.

A more complex relationship arises in respect of individuals who, not for compensation, provide copies of software to the victim without knowledge that the software has been infected by a virus. Since there is no commercial gain to the person providing the software, it is less clear that there is the same sort of duty to exercise the care described here.

A Bulletin Board System (BBS) operator provides a means by which users may communicate on issues of interest and share information, ideas, data, or software. BBS operators make their systems available to others who expect to rely on those systems. As a result the BBS operator may have a duty to screen uploaded software for virus contamination. At least the BBS operator should warn the users to exercise caution in using software downloaded from the BBS. A prudent BBS operator may seek to escape liability by making a limitation of his or her liability a condition of use of the BBS for all users.

The question of responsibility or liability for passing infected software is apart from the question of whether or not that software is infringing on the software developer's copyright. This factor, however, may be considered by the Court in assessing the relative strengths of the case by each party.[6]

As a potential victim, there are some things you might do to improve your legal position in respect of a possible virus infection, that is, to improve legal vaccines.

Improving Legal Vaccines

For one thing, you may be able to review the agreements under which software, maintenance service, and upgrades are acquired. You may be able to obtain warranties from BBS operators, retailers, or software developers that certain steps have been taken to protect acquired software from virus contamination. It may be worth paying a bit extra for software that a developer, dealer, or retailer is willing to warrant as virus free. You should also examine the warranties and terms under which you acquire programs. Future upgrades and the programs used in the screening process must be subjected to the same level of testing to ensure that the software stays free of infection.

Passing Laws

A typical reaction when society faces a new phenomenon is to cry "there ought to be a law" as though the mere enactment of legislative control or sanctions will resolve the problem. As noted earlier, the problem of virus creation and

---

[6]Some legal remedies may be unavailable or difficult to obtain if the victim who claims the remedy also has "unclean hands."

contamination is a broad social one that can only be addressed successfully on many fronts. Legal regulation or sanction is only one of those fronts.

One problem is that laws take time to enact. Legislators typically are not trained in technical matters, and they have many matters that seem to command top priority already. It may require months or years to create and pass a law. Enforcement through the courts involves lengthy investigations and trials and requires prosecutors and attorneys who understand the phenomenon so as to bring the action or prosecution. A computer virus may be conceived and created in a few hours, introduced into systems in seconds, and spread very widely in days or even minutes.

For the last decade, there have been law reform efforts in many jurisdictions introducing many specific criminal provisions dealing with unauthorized use of computer systems, intentional interference with data, and the like. This book makes no attempt to summarize all of these efforts. In reviewing this matter, we've chosen a specific example of such legislation. In addition, you should review the appropriate legislative provisions in your jurisdiction and, where appropriate, consult with an attorney with some experience in the area of computer law and computer crime for more specific information (Figure 10.2).

Criminal Liability

Criminal law is used by society whenever a certain form of conduct is so outrageous or so damaging to society as a whole that it is necessary for the massive power of the State's criminal justice apparatus to be brought into play. In this way, criminal law serves to punish offenders and to deter the potential future spread of computer viruses.

For information purposes, we'll use two examples of computer crime laws in the Criminal Code provisions for Canada, which provide uniform law throughout the nation. In the United States, criminal law is made both at the state and the federal level.[7]

In Canada, criminal law is entirely at the federal level; thus only one set of laws has to be considered, the Criminal Code of Canada. There are many potential criminal remedies; the most likely to be used are Section 301.2 (dealing with unauthorized use of a computer system) and Section 387(1.1) (dealing with mischief in relation to data). These sections came into force in December 1986.

---

[7]In January of 1988, a federal Computer Crime Act came into force and there is a model computer crime law available from the Data Processing Management Association that many states have used as a guide. A law banning computer viruses was introduced into the House of Representatives in July. Many complexities of jurisdiction arise, however, and these would unnecessarily complicate our book.

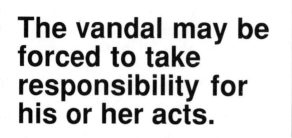

The vandal may be forced to take responsibility for his or her acts.

Figure 10.2 Responsibility

Unauthorized Use of a Computer

In many jurisdictions, and under Section 301.2 of the Criminal Code of Canada, the unauthorized use of a computer system may be a criminal offense. It seems likely that the act of introducing a virus into someone's computer initially would be considered to be unauthorized use of a computer, by causing the computer to perform unapproved acts (the reproduction of the virus and whatever nasty things it does when triggered).

A recent prosecution in the United States may be of interest. In Fort Worth, Texas, a computer programmer has been charged with deleting over 160,000 files from his former employer's computer by infecting it with a virus.[8] Newspaper reports indicate that the indictment accuses the defendant of executing programs "designed to interfere with the normal use of the computer" and acts "that result in records being deleted." The 160,000 records were sales commission data for employees of the company. Both charges would fall either under unauthorized use or mischief in relation to data discussed in the next section.

---

[8] See [Virus 1988]

Mischief in Relation to Data

The criminal code provision states the following:

Everyone commits mischief who wilfully

(a) Destroys or alters data;
(b) Renders data meaningless, useless or ineffective;
(c) Obstructs, interrupts or interferes with the lawful use of data; or
(d) Obstructs, interrupts or interferes with any person in the lawful use of data or denies access to data to any person who is entitled to access thereto.

Since most forms of computer virus infection involve some alteration of data, and the effect of a virus may either destroy or alter data, render data meaningless, useless, or ineffective, or obstruct, interrupt, or interfere with the lawful use of data, this section may be very appropriate for most virus prosecutions. Unfortunately, since the phenomenon is relatively new, there are few cases to rely on.

In one case, defendants encrypted data, making it useless for the rightful owner.[9] The court noted that the defendants' conduct could fall under the provisions of the (then-draft) Section 387(1.1).

Civil Liability

Civil law provides rules governing individual relationships. It provides no specific or immediate cause of action for placement of a computer virus in a host program with the view that it will be used and spread by an innocent user. Rather, we must look at the various theories under which an action may be brought at civil law. There are numerous variations that could be examined depending on the nature of the virus and the precise injury done. We will not look at some of these, such as intentional interference with economic relations or defamation and the like. Here we will focus on a brief review of the following:

1. Intentional interference with legitimate use;
2. Negligence; and
3. Strict liability.

As noted above, this is not to deny the possibility that additional actions might be brought under different theories.

---

[9] Turner v. The Queen, in Ontario in 1984.

Interference with Legitimate Use

Our law provides rules intended to protect our ownership and use of property. For example, if you buy a diskette and someone takes it without your permission then the law provides a means to get your diskette back. The law also protects the right of the person entitled to use a computer program. Intentional or deliberate interference with the users' rights may be the basis of a legal action.

When a person takes control of your diskette, as in the example above, the law requires that person to return it to you undamaged or to pay you its value. Where a virus takes control of program or data files and makes them either inaccessible or unusable to the user, the vandal creating the virus may be held accountable for the damage he or she has done.

Negligence

Civil liability emphasizes individual responsibility to the victim of the injury. There appears to be no doubt that the vandal who propagates a computer virus is, or should be, aware of the injury he or she is inflicting on innocent third parties. The law has, in the area of tort law, several types of action that might be used in a civil lawsuit against the vandal in cases in which specific intent may be less easy to prove.

Perhaps the most important basis to make a claim, where a specific intent to injure the victim may be difficult to prove, is negligence. Negligence has been described as having six elements, all of which must exist for liability to attach to the defendant:[10]

1. The claimant must suffer some damage;
2. The damage suffered must be caused by the conduct of the defendant;
3. The defendant's conduct must be negligent, that is, in breach of the standard of care set by law;
4. There must be a duty recognized by law to avoid this damage;
5. The damage should not be too distant or unconnected to the defendant's conduct; and
6. The conduct of the plaintiff should not be such as to bar his recovery, that is, he must not be guilty of contributory negligence and he must not voluntarily assume the risk.[11]

---

[10] A *defendant* is the person being sued; a *claimant* or *plaintiff* is the person suing another.

[11] Linden, *Canadian Tort Law* 4th edition, Butterworth's.

There appears no doubt that damage is suffered by the victim of a virus attack (points 1 and 2). Even if the virus only consumes memory space and causes inconvenience and frustration for the victim, there is a time cost, and perhaps third-party costs, associated with removing the virus from the system; some injury is done. It also seems clear that the damage suffered not only is caused by the defendant but is directly caused by the defendant's conduct. There appears to be no reason why a victim should not be able to claim for compensation against the wrongdoer. The only issues, if any, deal with the duty at law and the standard of care necessary to satisfy that duty.

The issue of distance from damage (point 4), has been addressed in a number of cases in law.[12] The basic rule is that persons who know or ought to know that a virus will be widely distributed and may have damaging or serious effects have a duty to those persons whose systems are infected. This duty may extend to the whole class of PC users but might not, for example, extend to mainframe users since there is little chance of that same virus spreading in the different and more secure mainframe operating system. The bottom line is that it appears clear that the vandal is or ought to be considered a neighbor of the owner and user of the innocent host program, within the meaning of the neighborhood principle. As a result, the vandal who contemplates spreading a computer virus has a duty of care in respect of those owners and users (points 3 and 5).

Once a duty of care is established, it is necessary to determine what standard the law requires to meet that duty. We submit that the conduct involved in creating and spreading a computer virus is intentional or, at least, completely reckless with a disregard for the interests and damage done to the victims of the act. The standard of care thus must be that a computer virus not be attached to a program in circumstances in which innocent users will gain access to the infected software and thus allow the virus to propagate.[13]

A clear consequence of the above arguments is that the vandal who introduces a computer virus into a computer system should be liable to the entire class of victims who are reasonably expected to be injured by the spread of the virus.

Point 6 regarding contributory negligence should be considered by potential victims. A court may not look with favor at a plaintiff who exposed himself or herself to a virus by means of a pirate copy of a program, for example, when certain forms of relief are sought. This is not to say that no remedy is available,

---

[12]The classic case is Donoghue v. Stevenson, 1932.

[13]There will, of course, be cases in which scholars and researchers, studying the effects of computer viruses or attempting to develop antiviral tools, will introduce a computer virus into a test system. We believe that the standard of care in such cases requires the strictest containment strategy so as to avoid contamination of other computer systems.

but rather that the plaintiff's own conduct may have limited the range of remedies available.

Strict Liability

Under legal precedent[14] as expanded for modern situations, people who introduce inherently abnormally dangerous processes, chemicals, objects, or devices into commerce or otherwise are often strictly responsible for any damage that results as a consequence of the inherently dangerous process.

There appears little doubt that the introduction of possible random damage or injury into a computer system without any regard to the consequences or type of computer system results in a certain inherent risk of danger to property. As we've noted in earlier chapters, in some cases, such as in those where computer systems govern health, safety and the like, a virus may result in or cause personal injury or death. Patient treatment records, traffic controls, air traffic control, industrial process control, and so on, are examples that come to mind easily (Figure 10.3).

We believe that in such cases, a standard of strict liability and absolute responsibility should be applied to the vandal introducing the computer virus into the host computer system. We believe as well that the fact that the injury caused in a computer system several generations removed from the initial innocent host system was not foreseeable should be no defense.

It is precisely the nature of a computer virus program that it will spread and reproduce without restriction to a wide variety of systems that the vandal cannot precisely predict. There is fundamentally a character of recklessness and complete disregard of the interests of others in the introduction of a computer virus program into an innocent host program.

---

[14]Ryland v. Fletcher, 1868 or modern product liability case law.

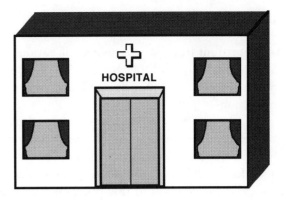

Real damage can be done by a virus attack

Figure 10.3 Viruses Can Be Life-Threatening

What Is to Be Done?

There are several significant problems with civil law actions. First, in most cases there will be a large class of individual victims, none of whom individually may have the resources to investigate and prosecute a civil action properly. Here the role of class actions may be very useful in bringing civil actions. A second problem with civil action for compensation is more fundamental. In many cases, the vandal has or may have little property or money with which to compensate the victims. It is a unique feature of our advanced technological society that such disproportionate damage or harm may be done to countless victims by persons who have no realistic prospect of compensating or making right the injury they do. As a result, we submit that the criminal law is more appropriate in dealing with computer virus cases.

Moreover, since the conduct being considered is extremely dangerous anti-social activity that results in intentional injury to innocent third parties and attacks the basis of security of modern business, governmental and other computer systems, the law, specifically the criminal law, has a role in providing a strong and significant deterrent to this type of conduct. The damage done by these people is of such magnitude and such broad consequence to the security of our entire society that a strong deterrent message must be sent (Figure 10.2).

SUMMARY

As is apparent from the discussion of various legal remedies, the legal system has not caught up with phenomena like computer viruses. Nevertheless, there are existing laws that may be used, and new laws are being enacted in various jurisdictions.

The phenomenon of computer virus contamination of software and the extraordinarily rapid spread of computer virus programs throughout many diverse computer systems is a significant threat to the reliability of all of our computer and telecommunication systems. As in dealing with any other kind of pandemic, the solution to this problem is not simple, and completely effective partial solutions will not be implemented in a short period of time. At this stage, it appears that the computer industry will have to rely on a combination of technical solutions (antiviral programs and various screening methods), the deterrent effect of prosecutions both civilly and under criminal law of vandals who introduce computer virus programs into computer systems, and an educational approach focussing on responsibility and ethics in the computer industry. The tasks involved are not minor, but neither is the threat to our computer systems. It is important that we begin immediately to take the first steps toward the solution of this problem.

In short, the message to potential vandals is that it is not just a lark or a harmless prank to spread a computer virus. *Don't do it!*

Chapter 11

RESPONSIBILITIES

I don't care who I damage. I don't care how much damage I do. I don't care how many jobs are lost or how many people are hurt when I'm triggered. Besides, why should I? I'm only a program; someone else loaded and pointed me and made me pull the trigger.

Ethics can be a slippery subject. We'll approach it by reviewing the motivations of the kinds of unethical people who intentionally spread computer diseases: vandals and terrorists. The we look briefly at relations between the law and ethics as they apply to computer viruses and professionalism. We close this chapter with an example of professional ethics: our own dilemma in writing this book.

UNDERSTANDING THE PHENOMENA

The description at the beginning of this chapter could apply equally to a bomb thrown by a terrorist or to a person who places a computer virus specifically designed to damage or injure the victims into a computer system. In the case of the terrorist, the motivation is often claimed to be political but also includes the desire for self-importance and the ability to project power over others (notwithstanding that the victims are innocent so that there is no real contest). The motivations of the vandal in designing and releasing a computer virus are complex and will vary form case to case. There are, however, some factors that recur in a number of cases. These are the desires to project power over others, to assert some effect from one's individual existence in the face of an increasingly complex and impersonal world, and the challenge to "see if I can do it," as well as a technical challenge, to defeat attempts to make systems impregnable.

Many of these factors point to a profile of a vandal who is socially alienated with a sense of powerlessness and inferiority, similar to conventional vandals in our society: those who damage or deface public property, torture or maim animals, abuse or bully small children, and the like.

THE VICTIM'S VIEW

So far, we've described how a virus works, some things to do about viruses, and some legal considerations. Each chapter begins with a thought that might represent the perspective of a virus in operation. Most of our attention has been on the virus and the perpetrator. But ethics includes considering more than one side of a conflict, and the victim has been neglected. The following material is abstracted from reports that were distributed by public BBSs about the Lehigh virus and about the PLO virus in Israel. These reports have been chosen from longer segments, but have not been edited otherwise; the grammatical and spelling errors may help indicate the sense of panic and helplessness that victims felt when they produced these warnings.

```
*************** MS/DOS Virus Warning ***************

Last week, some of our student consultants discovered a
virus program that's been spreading rapidly thoughout
Lehigh University.  I thought I'd take a few minutes
and warn as many of you as possible about this program
since it has the chance of spreading much farther than
just our University.  We have no idea where the virus
started, but some users have told me that other
universities have recently had similar problems. . . .

I urge anyone who comes in contact with publicly
accessible (sp?) disks to periodically check their own
disks.  Also, exercise safe computing--always were a
write-protect tab. :-) . . .

This is not a joke.  A large percentage of our public
site disks has been gonged by this virus in the last
couple days.

Kenneth R. van Wyk, User Services Senior Consultant,
Lehigh University Computing Center
```

[The following is translated from an article that appeared on "Maariv" (one of Israel's most popular daily newspapers) in 8-Jan-1988. The translator's comments appear in brackets '[]' within the translated text.]

The computer virus that got the nickname "the Israeli Virus" continues to run wild. The Hebrew University in Jerusalem spread the warning yesterday: Don't use your computer on Friday, the 13-th of May this year! In this day the virus was programmed to wake up from its hibernation - and destroy any information found in the computer memory or on the disks. Because of this reason, it also got the nickname "time bomb". Moreover, every 13-th of each month, the virus will cause a significant slow-down in the computer's response.

Evidences were received by Maariv yesterday for the existence of the virus in many other places in addition to the Hebrew University in Jerusalem. It was also reported to be detected in one of the I.D.F. [Israeli Defense Forces] units using personal computers.

Currently, the Hebrew University spreads immunization programs that enable detected the virus in the computer memory and exterminate it. A new problem popped up though: A mutation of the virus may show up, a few times as dangerous as the current virus. It all depends on the source of the virus and whether the person responsible for it is some computer wizard who did it for fun or some psychopath who does not control his moves.

The computer community is grateful for stopping the
process of unauthorized copying of software that
reached incredible use lately. Exactly like AIDS, that
generated the safe sex phenomenon, the computerized
virus is about to generate the phenomenon of decent use
only of software.

(by Tal Shahaf)

THE VIRUS REACHED HAIFA

The "Israeli virus" was detected, after causing much
damage also in the educational center of the ministry
of education in Rotenberg building on the Carmel
[mountain in Haifa]. There is a computer project going
on this site, in which tens of students participate.
The center manager, Gideon Goldstein, and the project
people Michael Hazan and Gadi Kats, told that 6 weeks
ago there was a virus discovered, which destroyed 15
thousand dollar worth software and 2 disks in which
7000 hours of work had been invested, in an
irrecoverable way.

(by Reuven Ben-Zvi)

PANIC AMONG OWNERS OF PERSONAL COMPUTERS

The Israeli virus panic moved from within the campus
and spread out also to the computer consumers in
Jerusalem. In many stores there were customers
reporting symptoms in their home computers, that
matched those which had been found in the P.C. systems
in the university. "This morning we ran into and heard
about a few cases", told Emanuel Marinsky, manager of
computer services lab, "It raises panic".

(by Arie Bender)

ETHICS

As we discussed in Chapter 10, the law provides sanctions against the vandal's conduct. There are civil sanctions requiring compensation for any injury done to victims and criminal sanctions providing a deterrent by threat of loss of liberty, payment of fine (in some cases, compensation to victims), and the continuing disruption of life as a result of a criminal record. It seems clear that in the coming years as virus attacks become more vicious and result in more damage, legal action will be brought against the vandals both civilly and under the appropriate criminal or penal codes.

Deterrent by threat of legal action alone (Chapter 10) is not the only answer. It is important that the computer industry and society generally confirm its abhorrence of a vandal's conduct. It is also important that the computer industry continue to encourage the development of professionalism and responsible conduct for its members.

Questions of ethics and responsibility must be addressed in the educational system, specifically in computer education classes. Here, particularly, it is important that instructors of computer education classes provide role models of ethical and responsible conduct. Although this comment may seem idealistic in the face of the real budgetary and other pressures faced by the modern educator, we must ask ourselves what the costs are to society of *not* instilling a sense of ethical responsibility in people trained to use potentially dangerous technical skills. It is important that the role model emphasize responsibility and ethical conduct.

PROFESSIONALISM

Some of the comments above are more appropriate to the young person moving through the educational system and his or her instructor than to the computer professional. The computer professional has a significantly higher level of responsibility. This is because the computer industry provides his or her livelihood, and the products of the computer industry have untold impact on society.

In some of the reported instances of computer sabotage (including some examples of virus attacks), the perpetrator is a former employee or consultant disenchanted or unhappy with the employer or former employer. The law provides several mechanisms to deal with these types of disputes. The sabotage of computer systems is not an acceptable response. This is particularly true for programmers, systems analysts, and other computer professionals who are or ought to be aware of the injury they do not only to their former employer but also to the integrity and structure of the computer industry as a whole.

Associations of computer professionals maintain standards of expectations for ethical conduct. We believe that actions of the kind discussed above should be sufficient to result in a review of the computer professional's certification, whether Certified Data Processor, Certified Systems Professional, or Fellow of the British Computer Society, and of membership in professional societies such as Data Processing Management Association, Canadian Information Processing Society, or the British Computer Society. Such conduct appears a clear breach of the codes of conduct and practice of such Associations and of the professional certifications.[1] The act of apparent vengeance by the computer professional ultimately injures the professional and others.

AN ETHICAL DILEMMA

It is difficult to write a book about a problem such as computer virus contamination, software piracy, or the like. In these chapters, we have provided some understanding of the phenomena, not to encourage them, but so that more meaningful and effective countermeasures can be taken. Since providing such material potentially could aid others' unethical behavior, we also provided warnings both to the vandals and to potential victims. Also, we have selected certain details very carefully (e.g., the material about what viruses do in Chapter 3 and the pseudo-code for a virus in Chapter 5). The victims should know that there are reasonable and cost-effective steps they can take to minimize their vulnerability from computer virus attacks. The vandals should know that their conduct is unacceptable and they will face not only the weight of legal sanctions but also the disdain of their peers in the computer industry.

---

[1] In fact, at least one computer consultant lost his CDP because of unethical use of data and computer access gained during an assignment at a financial institution.

Chapter 12

WHAT NEXT?

Oh, that's old stuff, I know how to get around that! Do you think I'm still wet behind the ears? I can even change myself so that my copies are invisible to your probes. I'm not dumb, you know. I'm working to improve my lot just as you're working to make my life harder.

FUTURE PROBLEMS

Technical solutions to the virus pandemic will follow the same fate as technical solutions to software piracy, or, for that matter, military weapons development. There will be a continuing contest between the developers of new and more virulent strains of virus programs and the developers of new forms of antiviral programs. In effect the viruses will evolve so as to become immune to or undetectable by antiviral programs or even to attach themselves to and form part of the antiviral programs.[1] This is not to suggest that significant research and development of antiviral programs should be halted. Indeed, given the scale of the problem created by computer viruses, one can only encourage and support the development of new antiviral software tools as quickly as possible. In the meantime, slower and longer-lasting solutions such as education and legislation will have a chance to work.

We observe that the people who are at greatest risk of computer virus infection are those who make extensive use of pirate copies, download every new game or program from a BBS, and otherwise are in a high-risk group. In other words, high-risk people are those who do the kinds of things hackers

---

[1] The Brain virus and others do in fact take active steps to hide themselves from attempted diagnostic routines. Even our example virus in Chapter 5 takes some camouflaging actions. We encountered one instance of an infected antiviral product and have seen reports of others.

delight in. There is poetic justice here: The hackers causing the problems of software piracy and computer viruses are themselves the people most likely to be exposed to another virus vandal. Unfortunately many ethical computer users are also caught in the backlash.

There is a risk that the incredible growth of the information society will be brought to a halt by the spread of diseased programs, as the free love movement of the 1960's has died with the spread of AIDS. We hope this does not come about. If you practice safe hex, you should be able to continue sharing information, programs, problems, solutions, and whatever with your friends over the computer networks, without much risk of computer virus infection. Even if you're infected, following some of the practices we've described will let you cure yourself without much nuisance.

When things settle down after a few cycles of virus attack and antiviral response, the end result will likely be that viruses remain a risk but a controlled one. Just as we pay taxes partly to support police and just as we gladly devote computer resources to user-friendly computer interfaces, so we will pay the tax of devoting some of our computer capability to virus protection. Unlike the taxes we pay for governments, the price we will have to pay for reasonable computer security will continue to shrink as a fraction of the computer power available; moreover, the price will be an insignificant portion of the value received.

The free sharing of computer information has already changed our society in many ways. It has the potential of being the greatest revolution in work and social relationships in human history. Take precautions, certainly; but join the revolution.

FUTURE SOLUTIONS

Software Manufacturers and Dealers

This subsection is directed to the developer of computer software. The manufacturer of computer software, is put into a difficult position by the computer virus phenomenon. He or she is an innocent third party victim--but also is in one of the best positions to control much of the spread of viruses. Realistically, distributors and dealers can't do much about shrink-wrapped packages received from a manufacturer: They'd have to break the tamper-proof packaging even to test for virus infection. The manufacturer may also have legal responsibilities, as discussed in Chapter 10. The following list outlines practices that may fulfill the legal obligations, and help ensure that the social obligation to distribute good products to customers is met.

- First, the manufacturer should follow current research on viruses and protection methods. The manufacturer has the resources and technical skills to stay with research developments, where individual customers might not. Manufacturers need to know what the risks are, and to minimize the risks.

- Manufacturers must ensure that their own shops are clean. A developer probably can't be certain that *no* virus can creep into work without imposing controls so rigid that no development team could function;[2] but the manufacturer certainly *can* use the latest list of known viruses to scan *everything* that goes outside the doors. That 100 percent check of anything that might go out, combined with statistical testing to check for viruses not on the known list, will mean at least the developer doesn't contribute to virus spread. Any upgrades, any beta test samples, anything the manufacturer uploads onto a BBS, or whatever *must not be infected*.

- The manufacturer must also test exhaustively anything coming *into* the shop. This includes samples of problems that beta testers or customers may send in.

- At some point the master copy may go to an outside vendor for mass reproduction and possibly to another outside party for packaging. The third parties have the same responsibility the manufacturer has: to be *certain* they don't introduce a virus infection into material they've received. Remember that if there are infected products distributed, the developer or manufacturer will carry much of the blame and the cost of recalls and such. Work closely with outside parties to be sure that the virus problem does not crop up.

- Distribute software on 5 1/4-inch diskettes that don't have write enable notches in them, or 3 1/2-inch diskettes without write enable tabs. Then anyone wanting to sabotage the product not only will have to be able to re-shrink-wrap the packaging, but will need special methods to alter the data on the diskette.

- All packages should come in shrink wrap or other, better, tamper-proof packaging.

- If software is distributed by means of any public BBS, then be sure the BBS operator is aware that you want the product to *stay* free of disease.

---

[2]For example, development work involves frequent creation or altering of system files, program files and such. You can't be sure that *none* of such alterations are virus caused and still function. There can be a policy that no employee will take home a diskette or bring a diskette into your shop--but such a policy would be extraordinarily difficult to enforce and could seriously impact productivity.

Manufacturers or developers can gain more control over distribution, and perhaps some marketing information as well, by using standard encryption processes:

- Collectively or individually, be sure that a standard encryption or checksum or similar program is widely available (Figure 12.1); and
- Distribute software in encrypted form and distribute an encryption key created using the software serial number as part of the key, on return of a registration card. The user then can be certain that the decrypted software has not been corrupted during transmission.

ADVANTAGE: (1) Any transmission paths can be used, and the probability of corrupting two different paths used for the software and the key is insignificant; (2) The developer ensures receipt of marketing information when the user returns the registration to get the encryption key; (3) There is much improved control over piracy, and no liability for any pirate copies.

DISADVANTAGE: (1) Clumsy sales strategy is likely to turn off potential buyers; (2) There is a necessity to create *fast* response to registrations (months won't cut it).

- Give the user a simpler way to check for virus infection by sending out the checksum created for the master diskette. A checksum program could be distributed as public domain, in an advertisement, or by using a variation on the encryption key method described above.

ADVANTAGE: (1) The user can check the checksum and ensure that the software hasn't been altered somewhere in the distribution chain; (2) If the registration card method is used, there are much the same advantages and disadvantages as encryption; (3) The user can use the program immediately, at a slight risk of infection, and after receiving the checksum can determine that there is no disease.

DISADVANTAGE: Similar to the previous strategy, but less so. The checksum program would be exposed to contamination but many copies of it would lessen the chances of any one being infected or altered.

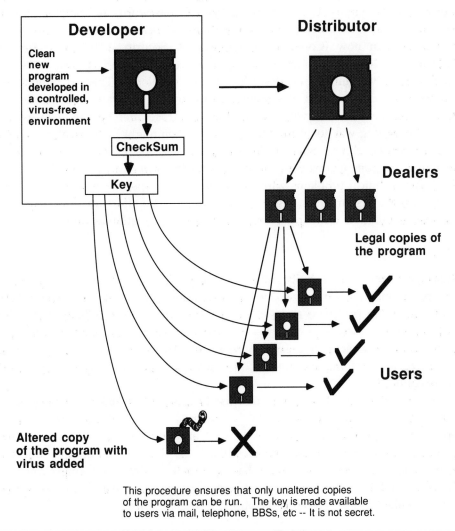

Figure 12.1 A Safe Software Distribution Technique

Many other variations on secure transmission methods can be and have been devised, and are in use today for things like EFT passwords and other situations in which security of transmission is important. Checksum programs are in the public domain now (Cohen in [Computers & Security 1988] for example). Admittedly, all such methods add some nuisance and may affect sales, and some methods imply significant expenses for you as a developer. These are among the unfortunate consequences of the spread of diseased software, and we all will have to learn ways to live with such problems. Viruses aren't going to go away.

An interesting way to address the virus situation might be for dealers to offer a virus testing clinic. Such a clinic could allow customers to test a newly acquired program against many antiviral products on a clean system. There are, however, technical problems with this concept: The operator would have to be very sure the system *stay*s clean,[3] for one thing. The effort involved might be expensive; but there is an opportunity for revenue generation as well.

Connectivity

Remember that connectivity includes many things that collectively make computers much easier to use, such as communications, compatible computers, and compatible programs and file structures. Connectivity is happening, and will continue to increase, simply because the whole is greater than the sum of the parts: More connectivity means more people freely communicating, sharing resources, and creating new things. The industry trends are very strong toward more connectivity.

Along with connectivity comes increased exposure to viruses, loss of privacy, and other potential problems. We've learned to live with explosive gases (propane barbecues, gasoline in cars, etc.) and we'll learn to cope with the problems we discover in computer connectivity. Like the automobile and the telephone, computer connectivity has so much potential for improving the human condition that the potential for good far outweighs the occasional problem like vandals who spread computer virus programs.

---

[3]The system would be exposed to any viruses brought in by legitimate customers--and also might become a target for vandals.

APPENDIX: SOFTWARE TO HELP WITH VIRUSES

This appendix lists a number of antiviral agents, separated into DOS and Macintosh products. Some of the products have been reviewed; some could not be reviewed within the publication deadlines for this book or for other reasons and are given as contacts only. Many of these products are available online from various BBSs and are in the public domain or are freeware or shareware. Prices for shareware are indicated where available. Since prices of commercial products are subject to change, they have not been included. The level of protection, ease of use, quality of documentation, and price vary considerably among these packages.

The reviews are not technical in nature. They take the position that any competently done product provides a measure of protection and that your prime considerations are cost and ease of use. Experience has shown that home or small corporate users normally will not put up with the level of nuisance necessary for really effective protection. Once a protection is defeated or not used, its value is nil; we feel that the average user is better off thinking about ease of use than about esoteric capabilities. A combination of common sense--safe hex--and use of any of these packages *as recommended by the producer* will provide considerable protection. *Note:* Like any other program, a vaccine may contain errors. Do not depend only on a vaccine and consider yourself perfectly safe. *No package provides complete protection.*

Dr. H. Highland of *Computers and Security* has reported that his team is engaged in a major research project for in-depth technical reviews, with a book forthcoming from Elsevier Science Publishers in early 1989. Those who have exposures to industrial espionage, national security concerns, or other more serious risks are advised to obtain copies of the planned technical book. Some preliminary results of his research have been published; see [Computers & Security 1988].

> *These reviews are preliminary and do not represent exhaustive testing. No warranty is implied or stated.*

Warning

> Virus protection products can be and have been targeted by the perpetrators of virus programs. If you download any such product from a public BBS, exercise precautions and test the product before installing or running it on your production system. We recommend that you obtain antiviral products directly from the developers.

We suggest you contact your favorite BBS and ask them what they're doing to prevent infection on the BBS and what products are available for user downloading. If they are not doing anything and don't have any such products, you may wish to reevaluate the exposure you incur by using that BBS. You can gain an increased measure of protection by obtaining several products and testing them against one another. While any single product may be infected, it is statistically unlikely that several products obtained from different sources all will be infected.

MS-DOS AND PC-DOS

The antiviral products for DOS typically fall into one of two groups:

- Tools that scan files for sensitive commands, text strings, or known virus code; and
- TSR programs that intercept sensitive DOS instructions.

The function of scanning for suspicious text strings is provided by many commercial utilities that allow you to scan a file. The first group of antiviral agents typically specialize; whereas the commercial utility does many other things as well, the antiviral agent only scans and reports problems to you. Some of the antiviral programs also look for known virus code or sensitive instructions, which is not something you would wish to do with a file edit utility. Some antiviral agents provide checksum or other signature capabilities.

Programs in the second group of DOS antiviral agents typically load themselves into memory in much the same manner as a virus or print spooler, using the TSR (Terminate and Stay Resident) call. They then block attempts by a virus to load itself or to issue sensitive instructions. Many provide the ability to make backups of sensitive data like FAT tracks, boot sectors, and CMOS.

Any of the TSR programs will consume some memory. They may interfere with your normal operation if you use tools like *Windows*, *Norton Utilities*, or other programs that legitimately utilize TSR and other sensitive instructions. TSR antiviral agents frequently interfere with each other if you attempt to load two or more. Since TSR virus protection programs intercept other programs' instructions, there is performance degradation. As a general rule, the more sophisticated (and expensive) a virus protection product, the better it is at allowing you to control these intercepts and minimize the effects of this sort of interference in your normal work. Remember TANSTAAFL: There's a price in convenience and dollars for protection from virus programs.

The tests performed simulated virus activity in the case of the TSR programs:

1.   Attempt to write to a .COM file;
2.   Attempt to write to a .EXE file;
3.   Attempt to write to COMMAND.COM;
4.   Attempt to write to FAT;
5.   Load another TSR program; and
6.   Look at Boot Track.

Programs that could scan for suspicious code were used to scan our production system and each other. None of the tested packages detected the infected copy of *FLUSHOT3*.

BOMBSQAD, CHK4BOMB, Andy Hopkins, Swarthmore Software Systems, 526 Walnut Lane, Swarthmore, PA 19081. Electronic BBS (302)764-7522. These are shareware, and the developer requests a payment of $10 if you retain and use them.

BOMBSQAD and *CHK4BOMB* are available from many public BBSs, including Greenberg's (see *FLUSHOT*). *CHK4BOMB* checks files for dangerous activities such as low-level DOS instructions and for ASCII text strings. *BOMBSQAD* is a TSR program that traps such low-level calls and allows you to permit them or stop their execution. Each comes with a two-page set of instructions sufficient to permit proper operation.

Our copies of *CHK4BOMB* and *BOMBSQAD* came from the same BBS that gave us the contaminated version of *FLUSHOT*, so we did not attempt to test them. Others report that these programs do what their documentation claims. Both have been around for a while, and no problems have been reported.

Disk Watcher, RG Software Systems, 2300 Computer Avenue #I-51, Willow Grove, PA 19090 (215)659-5300.

Disk Watcher, version 2.0, has had antivirus features added to a utility originally intended to provide useful protection and backup tools. This developed product comes in sealed containers, with professionally produced manuals. The virus manual is produced to the same standard, as an adjunct to the more comprehensive manual provided for *Disk Watcher*.

The material submitted for review included a white paper entitled Computer Viruses: A Rational Examination, which does a good job of discussing the situation without being too blatant a sales tool.

Disk Watcher's price is greater than some other tools that provide only virus protection; however, *Disk Watcher* is a professional product that does many other things as well. The original protection features, combined with the added virus features, successfully resisted our attempts to modify sensitive data. We did not test the disk management capabilities of the product.

Flushot, Software Concepts Design, Ross M. Greenberg, 594 Third Avenue, New York, NY 10016 (212)889-6438 (electronic BBS number). There is a registration fee if you retain and use the tool; Greenberg says that you can send a $10 contribution to a charity and the receipt to him.

Flushot Plus is available from Software Concepts Design as shareware. As often is the case with shareware, *Flushot Plus* has more features than some commercial software. It's a good product with excellent documentation, including a considerable discussion of what virus programs are and how they work. It successfully resisted our attempts to modify sensitive data. We rate *Flushot Plus* as a good buy.

WARNING

Some earlier versions of Flushot have become targets for vandals, and there are known to be copies of Flushot around that actually contain viruses and will infect you rather than protecting you. One that we obtained from a major publisher's BBS was named *FLUSHOT3*; we've heard reports of another named *FLUSHOT4*. The developer recommends that you use only *Flushot Plus*. We *strongly* recommend that you get it from the developer's BBS, which he guarantees to have an uninfected version. His BBS also has versions of some other protection programs that Greenberg uses regularly and believes are uninfected (see *CHK4BOMB, BOMBSQAD*).

Mace Vaccine, Paul Mace Software, 400 Williamson Way, Ashland, OR 97520 (503)488-2322.

Mace Vaccine is intended to be used in conjunction with *Mace Utilities*. *Mace Vaccine* is fairly simple and includes only one page of documentation; its price is correspondingly low. The instructions are simple, clear, and sufficient. It successfully resisted our attempts to modify sensitive data.

Other commercially available utility packages such as *PCTOOLS* and *Norton Utilities* offer capabilities similar to *Mace Utilities*; it is not necessary to purchase another utility if one set is already available. Note that with any of these utilities it is possible to scan a file; if you scan a newly downloaded program and find a text string such as HA HA Gotcha, avoid running that program.

NTIVIRUS, Orion Microsystems, P. O. Box 128, Pierrefonds, Quebec, Canada H9H 4K8 (514)626-9234.

The package provides a single diskette and a short instruction manual. The manual includes little fluff and a fair bit of straightforward information about how viruses work and how *NTIVIRUS* works. The package provides some protection against a memory resident virus discovered during the operation of *NTIVIRUS*, incorporates a virus scan, and calculates signatures that permit you to keep your system safe once you ensure you have no viruses. (See [Pozzo 1986] if you're interested in the technicalities of this type of protection.)

Madjid Boukri seems to know what he's talking about. Consider that Boukri suggests that the authorization tables built by *NTIVIRUS* be renamed (using included capabilities) to protect against a virus specifically aimed at *NTIVIRUS*. The documentation contains a fair amount of useful detail if you're technically oriented. You'll need to know enough about DOS to be comfortable with creating .BAT files in order to make full use of this package.

The package successfully resisted our attempts to modify sensitive data. When it scanned our production system it reported possible virus activity in a file with an unusual structure, as it should have. It did not detect the virus in the infected copy of *FLUSHOT3*. A patch to fix a reported problem with PS/2 machines was forwarded to us and is now part of the package.

If your primary need is to keep your DOS environment clean, *NTIVIRUS* is a good buy.

Vaccine 2.0, WorldWide Data, 17 Battery Place, New York, NY 10004 (800)643-3000 ext. 123 or (212)422-4100.

Vaccine 2.0 contains three programs that check for known viruses (in .EXE or .COM files or the system files), create and check signatures, and maintain an approved TSR list and disk lockout. It's provided with very little documentation; what is there, however, is easy to follow, works correctly, and is all that is needed to run the program.

The package successfully resisted our attempts to modify sensitive data. When it scanned our production system it reported possible virus activity in a file with an unusual structure, as it should have. It did not detect the virus in the infected copy of *FLUSHOT3*. It should not interfere with your normal use of the computer once you've set everything up.

Vaccine, Version 1.2, FoundationWare, 2135 Renrock Road, Cleveland, OH 44118 (800)722-8737 or (216)932-7717

Vaccine, Version 1.2 is a comprehensive protection scheme intended for corporate markets. It requires a system administrator and is not so friendly as some other products, but it should provide a greater level of protection. We were not able to obtain a copy for review in time for publication.

Other DOS packages we did not test and have no reports on follow:

- *Antidote*, Quaid Software Ltd., 45 Charles St. East, Toronto, Ontario, Canada M4Y 1S2;
- *Antigen*, Digital Dispatch, Inc., 1580 Rice Creek Road, Minneapolis, MN 55432;
- *C-4*, Interpath Corporation, 4423 Theeney Street, Santa Clara, CA 95054;
- *Cryptographic Checksum*, Dr. Fred Cohen, University of Cincinnati, Dept. of Computer Engineering, Mail Location 30, 898 Rhodes Hall, Cincinnati, OH 45221-0030;
- *Data Physician*, Digital Dispatch, Inc., 1580 Rice Creek Road, Minneapolis, MN 55432;
- *Disk Defender*, Director Technologies, Inc., 906 University Place, Evanston, IL 60201;
- *Dprotect*, Gee Wiz Software Company, c/o: Ms. Janey Huie, 10 Manton Avenue, East Brunswick, NJ 08816;
- *Dr. Panda Utilities*, Panda Systems, 801 Wilson Road, Wilmington, DE 19803;
- *Novirus*, Digital Dispatch, Inc., 1580 Rice Creek Road, Minneapolis, MN 55432;
- *Vaccine*, Sophos Limited, 20 Hawthorne Way, Kidlington, Oxford OX5 1EZ, U.K.;
- *Vaccinate*, Sophco, PO Box 7430, Boulder, CO 80306;

  Sophco reported that the virus product had been sold to another company. We were not able to get further information in time for publication.
- *VI-Raid*, Prime Factors, 1470 East 20th Avenue, Eugene, OR 97403;
- *Viralarm*, Lasertrieve, Inc., 395 Main Street, Metuchen, NJ 08840; and
- *VirusSafe*, ComNETco, Inc., 29 Olcott Square, Bernardsville, NJ 07924.

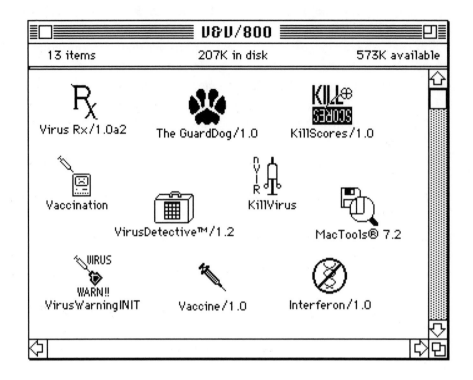

Figure A.1 Icons of Some Macintosh Antiviral Products

MACINTOSH

In general, Macintosh antiviral agents fall into one of four categories:

- Applications that can be launched and will perform some diagnostic and/or treatment function on files that may already be infected;
- Desk Accessories that function in a manner similar to applications but have all the advantages and limitations inherent in DAs;
- INITs that patch the System at boot time and offer some active protection against infection; and
- cdevs that behave in a manner similar to INITs but offer the added flexibility of user control from the Control Panel.

The INITs and cdevs are only useful with System Version 5.0 and later. They are installed by placing them on the System Folder.

The antiviral products reviewed below may perform differently under different Systems on the Macintosh. We have tested them under System 4.2, Finder 6.0 (System Software version 5.0) under the Finder. No testing was performed under MultiFinder.

As with DOS TSR antiviral agents, there may be undesirable interaction between antiviral INITs and cdevs and other cdevs or INITs in your System or other antiviral agents.

Copy II for the Apple Macintosh, Central Point Software, #200 - 15220 NW Greenbrier Parkway, Beaverton, OR 97006, (503)690-8090

> *Copy II for the Apple Macintosh* is a set of programs designed to help recover files that have been destroyed, accidentally or otherwise. The utilities work on the basis that when files are damaged or deleted, often the addresses of the pieces of the file are lost but the actual data remain intact. Since one common form of virus damage is to damage or destroy the tables listing where the pieces of files are stored, these tools may help in recovering from virus damage. Most of the tools can be used in two modes: in a turnkey (automatic) fashion for the average user, and as exploratory utilities for more knowledgeable users trying to repair damage.

A set of tools with similar capabilities for DOS machines is *CopyIIPC*.

The most useful of the tools are:

- *CPSSaveDeletes*: an INIT that automatically keeps track of the location and contents of files as they are deleted. For this utility to be of value, it must be installed before deletions on the disk to be protected. This protection could be valuable as a level of protection against viral attack.

- *CPSTagFix*: an INIT that automatically patches the Mac Plus and 512KE ROMS so that they write reliable tags on all diskettes and some hard disks. (Tags are useful when trying to recover deleted files.)

- *MacTools*: an application that allows a user to examine and perhaps recover some or all of the contents of deleted files. It offers three different methods of recovering deleted files, each of which relies on different information on the disk.

Ferret, Larry Nedry (address unavailable).

Available on several bulletin boards. This application is reported to detect and kill the SCORES virus and repair damaged files. Some of the corrected programs may fail to reboot properly; Adobe *Illustrator* and Adobe *Pagemaker* are reported as being particularly difficult to repair. Should this occur, your only recourse is to use backups or the original program disks.

Version 1.1 of *Ferret* has been reported to have a serious bug. It apparently does not delete one of the virus resources nor inform the user of the omission. Version 1.0 is reported to delete all the virus resources correctly but may have problems correctly identifying infected files.

GuardDog, Nemesis Systems, P.O. Box 33268, Minneapolis, MN 55433. *GuardDog* is shareware, and the author requests a $20 payment if the package is retained and used.

This unique cdev is not truly an antiviral agent but rather is in the nature of an activity control measure. The package allows the user to modify the manner in which the Finder moves, deletes, copies, or renames files or folders. Such activity can be prohibited or restricted. People attempting to initiate prohibited activities provoke a loud and distinctive audible alarm and are blocked.

Some of the features of *GuardDog* use the Control key, available only on Mac SE and Mac II keyboards.

Interferon, Robert Woodhead, c/o Robert Woodhead Sir-Tech Software, 10 Spruce Lane, Ithaca, NY 14850. *Interferon* is shareware; the author requests that you send an appropriate donation to the Vision Fund, c/o the above address if you retain and use it.

Interferon is a sophisticated antiviral application 12K in size that comes with a complete and informative user manual in *MacWrite* format. It is designed to detect and destroy several viruses, including SCORES and nVIR, and to detect anomalies that may be attacks from new, unknown virus programs. As with DOS, such anomalies may be intended activities of legitimate programs, and *Interferon* therefore allows you to control this feature.

Two features limit the usage of *Interferon*. The package cannot scan MFS (Macintosh File System) disks, only HFS (Hierarchical File System) disks. If the user chooses the eradicate option, *Interferon* does not remove the virus but *destroys* any file in which it detects a virus (this is documented in the accompanying manual).

Kill Scores, Howard Upchurch of MacPack, and Apple Corps of Dallas. MacPack is at P. O. Box 832446, Richardson, TX 75083.

Detects and eradicates the SCORES virus and restores damaged files and the System as much as possible. A comprehensive report is generated indicating what the package detected as it scanned the selected folder or disk.

Online documentation is provided. No indication is given in the documentation as to whether this is freeware, shareware, or a commercial product.

KillVirus, Matthias Urlichs, Rainwiesenweg 9, 8501 Schwaig 2, West Germany.

KillVirus is an INIT designed to combat the nVIR virus. The package deletes the resources of the virus from the system and attempts to prevent further infection by installing a dummy resource that looks like the virus (a new copy will find one of itself already there and remain dormant).

This dummy resource looks like the nVIR virus to other antiviral agents; if they attempt to clean up the "infected" file, unpredictable results may occur.

No documentation was received with the copy downloaded for review. There is no indication whether this tool is freeware, shareware, or commercial.

Vaccination and *VirusWarn*, Mike Scanlin, P. O. Box 400, Placentia, CA 92670.

The product is composed of two parts: the *Vaccination* application and the *VirusWarn* INIT.

The *Vaccination* application targets only the nVIR virus and can vaccinate only application files, not System files or other types of files. Files to be investigated are chosen one at a time from the SFGetFile dialog box. *Vaccination* removes nVIR but does not prevent future infection.

The *VirusWarn* INIT will beep to warn you should the nVIR virus attempt to infect your System. This is a warning only; the INIT does not block the infection.

The reviewed copy was downloaded and came with no documentation, no online documentation, no version number, and no indication as to whether it is freeware, shareware, or commercial.

Vaccine, CE Software, 1584 Fuller Road, West Des Moines, IA 50265.

Vaccine is a cdev offered free to the general public. CE software will provide it on a guaranteed clean disk, along with other CE Software products, for a fee of $10. The current version is 1.0 and there are no plans for future upgrades.

Vaccine is reported to offer protection against SCORES, nVIR, and the *MacMag* virus. It works by intercepting suspicious actions such as attempting to modify system resources. Since such activity can be a legitimate result of the use of a tool like the *Installer* or the *Font/DA Mover*, *Vaccine* can be turned on and off from the Control Panel.

Extensive on-line documentation is provided. No detailed Macintosh knowledge is needed to implement *Vaccine*, and it is transparent when in use. The documentation includes limitations of *Vaccine* and a short course in CE Software's very professional approach to virus control.

In expert mode, a very small icon appears in the upper right-hand corner of the screen if an anomaly is detected. To permit or block the anomalous activity, the user must click the appropriate button; but the pointer stays as the watch cursor and the hot point appears to be in the center of the watch face. This makes it difficult to select the correct button, and selecting the wrong button could be disastrous.

VirusRx, Apple Corporation, Inc.

VirusRx is provided at no charge by Apple and may be available from your local Apple dealer as well as from BBSs. The material reviewed was version 1.0a2; documentation revision date April 25, 1988.

VirusRx consists of a 12K application with extensive documentation as a separate file. The application will scan user directories or disks and provide an extensive report on problems detected. No attempt is made to remove virus programs or to repair any damage discovered. The documentation is an integral part of the package. Apple offers excellent advice to follow when investigating suspect software and suggests several precautions users can take to minimize their exposure to computer viruses.

Virus Detective, Jeffrey S.Shulman, P. O. Box 521, Ridgefield CT 06877-0521.

Virus Detective is a 23K Desk Accessory that allows a user to scan for various file components that may be part of a virus. The current version is 2.3, and the package is shareware with a $15 payment to the author requested if the package is kept and used.

Virus Detective is geared toward experienced Macintosh programmers. It allows the user to instruct the package to scan for resources of a particular type or creator, size, size range, or name. Offending resources can be removed. Some templates are provided by the author to help less experienced users get started.

Good online documentation is provided, including instructions for configuring the package and modifying the search criteria. A comprehensive report can be generated in any of several word processor formats, and the user can specify a directory or an entire disk to be scanned.

GLOSSARY

Add-on Card In personal computers, it is common to purchase and install cards that enhance the capability of the machine. Examples include built-in modems, graphics cards for color or high-resolution displays, clocks, and expanded memory.

BBS See Bulletin Board System.

Beta Test When software is developed, it must be tested. After the developer thinks the product is pretty good and has gone through his or her own testing process, it may be released to a limited group of people who will test the product in actual use. This second level of testing is called a beta test. It's important that the people in the beta test group be at arms length from the developer so they're motivated to find problems, not to prove the product works okay. Beta testing adds to the cost of the software and delays its release. Some developers are said to announce product availability when it goes to beta testers; see Vaporware.

Bitnet One of the many widely used mail systems, Bitnet links mostly universities and academics, and is worldwide in scope. It has the ability to transfer programs, either by means of translation programs or directly as executable files.

Boot Sector On a microcomputer disk or diskette, a particular location contains some simple code that allows the computer to begin the process of ".i.booting up." Booting up involves loading the operating system and starting operations. This location on disk or diskette is the boot sector. Note that some computers have a version of the system, often only a skeleton, in ROM (see ROM); these will start up and show a prompt with no diskette or hard disk available. If your computer does not have this ROM, you can't start it without a system disk or hard disk. The boot sector is a common target of viruses.

Bug An error in a program. Bug refers to unintentional errors, not to things like viruses and logic bombs. Adm. Grace Hopper, one of the pioneers in computer development, relates how the original computer "bug" was just that: A problem that turned out to be caused by a moth that had been squashed by a relay and acted as an insulator. There's a story that the original bug is in the Museum of Naval History; it may not be true, but it's certainly a good story.

Bulletin Board System (BBS) Computer that is run as an electronic "bulletin board." People can access the computer and put "notes" on the bulletin board, which anyone else with access can read. A BBS can be anything from someone's hobby to an international commercial BBS like CompuServe. The BBS concept is a key to the increasing connectivity available to people with computers, and also to the spread of useful programs, information--and viruses.

Commercial services may include such capabilities as listing products and allowing credit card purchases, information services such as the Official Airline Guide, and a host of other features.

CompuServe and The Source are commercial networks that are very widespread. Many computer-oriented magazines support their own systems. There are thousands of bulletin boards, one or more for every group of people with common interests and access to computers and communications. Some are free; some charge for usage. Some concentrate on such areas as how to break computer systems, how to make bombs, and so on. Most are more legitimate.

Checksum Number calculated based on the contents of a file. The calculation method varies, from adding up the numeric equivalents of each character (e.g., an ANSI uppercase "A" has the numeric equivalent of 65) to more sophisticated methods. CHECKSUM is also a communications protocol commonly used in microcomputer communications applications. If the checksum changes for a program, the program has changed and a virus (or a problem in the communication line in the other application) may be suspected.

Ciphertext When information is encoded, the coded result is unreadable without knowing the encryption key (see Encryption). The unreadable text is called ciphertext. See also Plaintext.

Clock One thing a computer needs to function is a clock. The clock allows the computer to synchronize things so they happen at the proper times. This synchronizing clock is built into every computer. One popular type of add-on board contains a clock with a battery backup; this clock is different from the one inside the computer, and mostly provides current date/time information after the computer has been turned off for a while.

CMOS (Complementary Metal Oxide Semiconductor) relates to how the transistors in an integrated circuit work. Microcomputer people misuse CMOS to refer to some storage related to the clock in the computer. Designers use it to retain certain information after the computer is switched off; since CMOS takes less power than some other kinds of transistors, batteries last longer. One example is add-on cards or other clocks that save the clock setting. Another example is found in ATs, PS/2s and Macintosh computers, where parts of the operating system and information about the computers' settings may be stored in CMOS. Some viruses have been reported to change the CMOS, becoming very hard to stop or get rid of, since this memory normally is not available to a user without specialized tools.

Connectivity More than simply the ability to call up and link to someone else's computer, connectivity takes in compatible software, standard formats, good telephone lines, satellite transmission, and many other things that collectively make it easier for anyone to "talk" to anyone else. It's actually possible for someone to use a cellular telephone in a car, with a laptop computer and portable modem, to call up a computer database in another country on an entirely different kind of computer.

Cryptanalysis *(See* Cryptography.)

Cryptography Discipline involving principles, means, and methods for changing data so that it is not readable. Encryption methods and principles are examples of things considered by cryptography. *Cryptanalysis* is an attack on one of the principles, means, or methods, such as decryption.

Decryption Process of transforming ciphertext back into plaintext.

Desk Accessory (DA) On the Macintosh system, a useful thing available to you from the DeskTop or from within an application. Examples include ways to change how your screen looks, calendars that remind you of appointments, calculators for arithmetic, and phone lists. Some programs on DOS machines, like *Windows*, *GEM*, and the *Presentation Manager*, have similar features.

Downloading Calling up another computer, bulletin board system (*see* BBS), or whatever, and copying a program or file from that system onto yours. (*See also* Uploading.)

Electronic Mail (e-mail) Passing messages along from one user of a computer network to another. Some mail systems can link to other networks and mail systems. They may have mailboxes, name and address lists, and other features. E-mail is becoming standard on large computer systems, and there are commercial services such as ATTMAIL and Envoy 100. Most of the commercial services allow transfer only of text data, so you can't send formatted word processor files or programs, only messages. BBSs normally have some kind of e-mail, usually for text only with separate capabilities for file uploading and down-loading.

Enciphering Process of changing information (plaintext) so that it becomes unreadable. There are many ways to do this; one involves using the Data Encryption Standard (DES). The resulting ciphertext is very difficult or impossible to read without the key used to encrypt it. Most enciphering methods also include something similar to a checksum, adding a level of protection and other benefits such as error correcting codes.

Encryption *See* Enciphering.

Exponent Mathematical entity that indicates that a number, the base, is raised to the power of the exponent. For example, in 10^5 the 5 is the *exponent*, and the 10 is the *base*. The expression is shorthand for 10 X 10 X 10 X 10 X 10 (10 multiplied by itself 5 times), or 100,000. Exponential refers to a kind of growth: If something doubles every time it reproduces, you have 1, then 2, then 4, then 8, then 16, then 32, and so on ($32 = 2^5$). Exponential growth can produce very large numbers very quickly.

Exposure A vulnerability, something in your computer or your method of operating that leaves you open to someone else doing things to you. (*See also* Point of Attack)

FAT (File Allocation Table) FAT is the name of part of the MS-DOS or PC-DOS operating system's ways to keep track of what's on a disk or diskette. Somehow, the computer needs to be able to find out what files are on a disk (the directory) and where all the pieces of a file are stored. The FAT, or something similar with a different name, is a specific part of a disk that is reserved. It contains the locations and sometimes sizes of all the parts of every file stored on a disk. If anything goes wrong with the FAT, the data may still be on a disk or diskette but the system can't find them. Some viruses make things go wrong with the FAT.

Firmware Programs that are stored in programmable read-only memory chips (PROM). It's possible to change firmware so it's not "hard" ware, but special tools are needed so it's not "soft" ware either. There's a progression from "software" to "firmware" to "hardware."

Fragmentation When there's a lot of file activity on a disk, eventually the clusters that contain the data will be scattered all over the storage space instead of being neatly located one after the other. This doesn't really hurt anything except for using up some storage for pointers to the locations of the next clusters and, because access to the file has to jump all over the place to find the clusters, slowing down file access. Since the slowing can be dramatic, disk reorganization programs are popular.

Freeware Programs distributed on bulletin boards without charge. (If there's a registration fee, it's called "shareware.") Many software manufacturers distribute upgrades or fixes for their programs this way.

FUBAR Acronym (possibly originally devised by the Egyptians while building pyramids or something). Let's just say that it stands for "*Fouled Up Beyond All Recognition*."

Garbageware Coined term used to refer to diseased programs (software) that contain and spread computer viruses, or otherwise are designed to damage things rather than to help you use your computer.

Hardware In computers, the part you can kick when you are frustrated.

LAN (Local Area Network) Computers can be linked into networks with various kinds of wires, cables, or electronic linkages. There may be many different computers, or even different kinds of computers, as well as printers, big disk drives called file servers, and other things in a network. A Local Area Network is one that is geographically close together, usually in one building or a small group of buildings. A LAN does not make use of public carriers in linking together its components (although it may have a "gateway" outside the LAN that uses a public carrier). (*See also* WAN.)

Logic Bomb Code put into a program that does something not intended or expected by the user. The logic blows up (activates itself) at some specific time, or because of some specific happening; otherwise, it does nothing except use up a bit of memory. A programmer could put a logic bomb into a program that causes damage if the programmer's name disappears from the payroll files, for example. A virus is one form of logic bomb, although a virus reproduces and logic bombs normally don't.

Plaintext (also cleartext) Original form (usually readable) of information or data. When you encrypt plaintext you get ciphertext.

Point of attack Specific vulnerability that a vandal is attempting to exploit to get into your system or to damage it. Chapters 5 and 7 mention several common points of attack where a virus tries to get into your system or attack to do damage.

RAM (Random Access Memory) What you normally think of as memory in your computer, for example the 640K of memory the computer has. (There also may be other memory that you as the user normally don't see.) You have to load a program into RAM before it can run, and you normally work on data in RAM.

Reverse Engineering Process by which computer people take a computer chip, or the machine-code executable version of a program, and figure out what the source code must have been to produce the program or the effects of the chip. Sometimes chips are examined physically to determine how they're created. The main reason to do this is that source code is much easier to read than the hex (base 16) numbers of machine code, and people can then devise other ways to do the same thing. The other ways to do the same thing may not be covered under the copyright or patent of the original developer of the chip or program. Reverse engineering is very common in computer applications, so much so that disassemblers, which take the object code and produce assembler code, are normal commercial products. It's one way to examine a virus program to see what it actually does, and how it does it.

Risk A measure of uncertainty. In information security, a risk is evaluated as a combination of exposures, plus points of attack, plus how likely an attack is, plus the cost to you of a successful attack. There are many ways to combine such elements to get numbers, and the numbers can then guide you in deciding where to allocate limited resources to minimize system risk.

Risk Analysis Formal process of identifying risks, determining how likely they are, determining potential losses, and coming up with numbers that are used as part of the process of deciding on a protection strategy.

ROM (Read-Only Memory) A form of memory in computers. The important difference is that you can't change ROM. There are variations such as programmable ROM (PROM) that can be changed, using special tools. Things like operating system kernels get stored in ROM where they're not vulnerable to errors or sabotage.

Safe hex Term we use to describe the whole group of common-sense practices that will help you avoid your system becoming infected with a computer virus program. It includes avoiding high-risk behavior like swapping pirate copies, doing things like keeping good backups so you can recover from an attack, and other procedures.

Shareware Programs distributed on bulletin boards for which the developers ask the user to send in money for a registration fee, or manuals, or the full-blown version of a demonstration program available on the BBS. Usually, the developer puts a page or two of copyright notices and such in front. This is one marketing strategy that has evolved to combat piracy: Let people copy the program, then ask them to be honest and send money, or offer them added value such as a manual or upgrades if they send money.

Signature Something unique about data that determines its characteristics. If the signature changes, the data have changed. If the data change, the signature changes. An example is the combination of the length of a file, with its exact name and whether it is read-only. If a virus adds something, or the file is changed from read-only to modifiable, the signature is different. For greater protection, a checksum can be computed as part of the signature (*see* Checksum). Complex methods of determining a signature are used in special cases. Vaccine programs often compute signatures, save them, and check them before loading a program as one way to find out if a virus has been around. If the program's signature has changed, it will not be loaded since it needs to be checked for possible virus activity.

Software   Programs you use or write. It's "soft" as opposed to firmware or hardware because software is easy to change.

Sysgen   Coined from *sys*tem *gen*eration, the process that systems people go through when setting up a mainframe operating system to reflect their particular configuration, choices, and so on. Because of the sysgen process, mainframe operating systems as installed are seldom identical. Note that there is no sysgen process for microcomputers; DOS is DOS anywhere. (The CONFIG.SYS file and some other techniques in DOS, or customizing the DeskTop or fonts on a Macintosh, can do something like a sysgen, but at a much simpler level.)

Traffic Analysis   One way of getting information about communications. Who calls, whom they call, how often, and when, are data that can provide useful information in traffic analysis. It may be useful to know, for example, that someone calls a specific number very often on Mondays and Fridays. If the someone is a bank manager and the number is for a bookie, traffic analysis has given a security manager a clue to a possible security exposure, without actually intercepting anything.

Trapdoor   Something in a program that lets a user do things (often, to get around normal security controls) by entering some special combination. A program for example, may execute normally, but when the programmer presses a certain combination of keys, the program opens a trapdoor into system files so that the programmer has access that normally would be denied. Another kind of trapdoor might be put into a system to allow unauthorized access to someone such as a fired employee. It has been common to have trapdoors left in mainframe operating systems so that systems programmers (who know the secret) can get into some kind of debug mode when things go wrong. This can be very convenient for the system programmer and also for a vandal who learns about the trapdoor.

Trojan Horse   In Homeric legend, the Greeks gained entry into Troy by concealing troops in a wooden horse that the Trojans took inside the city walls. In computer security, a Trojan Horse is an apparently useful program that does things in addition to what it's advertised to do. For example, it might be advertised as a disk compression utility, and it may indeed compress data on your disk. It might, however, also copy a virus into your COMMAND.COM file.

TSR (Terminate and Stay Resident) In DOS, a program can Terminate and Stay Resident. It stops executing and looks like it's gone, but remains at least partly in memory (memory resident), and can be brought up by pressing a special key. Examples include print spoolers, shell programs, and some clock programs. Pressing a function key might get you a clock display so you can check the time while you're working, without exiting from the working program. One way viruses get themselves executed is to issue a TSR; once in a while you press a key that lets the virus run, and it copies itself, or perhaps formats your hard disk. You might not notice it running when it merely copies itself.

Uploading When you contact another computer and transfer a file from your machine to the other computer, you are uploading. (*See also* Downloading.)

Vaccine Program, or group of programs, that provides some kind of protection against computer viruses. Often, one program checks files for known viruses and another TSR program stays around to trap any attempt by another program (such as a virus) to issue a TSR call or to format a disk.

Vaporware Coined term that refers to hardware or software that has been announced but not delivered. For example, "WonderWorks Version 99" may have been announced, several times, but nobody can buy it. Until it's actually available for sale and delivered, it's vaporware. The fact that people felt a need to invent this word may indicate something about marketing practices of some software and hardware developers.

Virus Program intended to do something in your system that you did not ask to be done. The key things that make it a virus are that it attaches itself to another program and it reproduces. What gives the computer virus its name is that it comes along with other programs similarly to the way a disease virus infects a cell and is reproduced when the cell reproduces. A virus can be benign, in which case it does no harm--perhaps only displays a "peace" message. Some viruses definitely are not benign. Since the virus makes copies of itself, when you discover it in one place, you have to check everywhere to be sure you're rid of it. It may lie dormant for a long time or merely reproduce for a while before doing its nasty thing.

In one sense, a virus is a Trojan Horse or logic bomb that replicates (copies) itself. The way a virus attaches itself to a program or otherwise hitches a ride may differ from one operating system to another.

WAN (Wide Area Network) Like a LAN, except that parts of a WAN are geographically dispersed, possibly in different cities or even on different continents. Public carriers like the telephone company are included in most

WANs; a very large one might have its own satellite stations or microwave towers. A WAN has exposures that are avoided in a LAN. (*See also* LAN.)

Wetware   After firmware, freeware, garbageware, hardware, shareware, software and vaporware, we couldn't resist defining this one. Wetware is people. We've heard about fantasyware and consumer compatible liveware (salesmen in computer stores) too.

Worm   Malicious program that worms its way through your computer, doing things like shifting bytes to garbage, or just overwriting them as it moves. The worm does not reproduce in the sense of producing new copies but does move itself around (a kind of reproducing) each time it does something. It can be very hard to find a worm even if you know it's there and doing damage. Many viruses are also worms.

REFERENCES

Attanasio, C.R., P.W. Markstein, and R.J. Phillips Penetrating an Operating System: A Study of VM/370 Integrity *IBM Systems Journal*, 15 No. 1, pp. 102-116.

Beeler, Jeffry System Break-ins Raise Concern Over Electronic Terrorism *Computerworld*, Nov. 24, 1986.

Benmergui-Perez, Marlene Your System: Safe and Sound? *Computing Canada*, Oct. 1, 1987, pp. 39ff.
> *An "Awareness" article reporting on general lack of effective security.*

Bornstein, Howard Viruses: Nothing to Sneeze At *Macintosh Today*, May 2 1988, p. 17.
> *An editorial discussing some of the potential problems with viruses in industrial espionage and national security areas.*

Bouros, Laz A Look at EDP Threat Assessment *Computing Canada*, Oct. 29, 1987, pp. 46ff.
> *A brief overview of a methodology for approaching threat, vulnerability, risk assessment used with some success by Canadian Federal Government. See [Fites 1988] for a more detailed treatment of similar methodology. See also RCMP Security Information series.*

Brandstad, Dennis K., Ed., Computer Security and the Data Encryption Standard, *National Bureau of Standards Special Publication 500-27*, 1978.

Browne, Malcolm W. Locking Out the Hackers *Discover*, Nov. 1983.

Bruschweiler, Wallace S. Sr. Computers as Targets of Transnational Terrorism, in *Computer Security: IFIP/Sec '85*, Elsevier Science Publishers, North-Holland.
> *Describes cases of bombings of computer centers in Europe and the United States. Includes samples from Red Brigade Manifesto regarding computer targeting.*

Chevreau, Jonathan Software Encryption: Protect Your Data *Computer Data*, May 1986.

Cohen, Fred Computer Viruses: Theory and Experiments *7th DOD/NBS Computer Security Conference*, Sept. 1984.

Computer Piracy and Privacy (Home of the Future: Industry Research Report series), The Yankee Group, Boston, 1984.

[Computer Security 1983] Case Histories in Computer Security, *Computer Security*, No. 53, Jul./Aug. 1983.

[Computers & Security 1988] *Computers & Security* 7 No. 2, Apr. 1988, Elsevier Advanced Technology Publications, Mayfield House, 256 Banbury Road, Oxford 0X2 7DH, England.

> *This issue concentrates on computer virus programs. The material is more technical than that in this book; this particular issue of is the single best easily available technical reference on computer virus programs at September 1988.*

[Computer Virus #1] Computer Virus--The Major Computer Abuse Threat of 1988? *The Computer Law and Security Report*, May-June 1988, pp. 2-3.

[Computer Virus #2] Computer Viruses: Software Armageddon? *Computer Dealer News*, 4 No. 11, June 2, 1988, pp. 1, 38.

[Computer Virus #3] Computer Viruses: The New Global Threat *The Computer Law and Security Report*, May-June 1988, pp. 2-3.

[Computing Canada 1988 #1] How Dangerous Are These Viruses? Computing Canada, Apr. 14, 1988, p. 10.

> *An editorial pointing out that fairly simple preventive measures avoid most exposure to viruses. The editorial indicates that virus programs represent unreasonable paranoia. (The infected copy of FLUSHOT3 described in the Appendix came from Computing Canada Online, this publication's bulletin board.)*

[Cortino 1988 #1] Cortino, Juli, and David Goll Apple Rallies Against Virus *Macintosh Today*, Apr. 19, 1988, p. 1.

> *Report of Apple's response to a virus in Dallas Texas, Landover Maryland, and government agencies in Washington D.C. See also [Cortino 1988 #2].*

[Cortino 1988 #2] Cortino, Juli Virus Concern Spurs Vaccines, Investigations *Macintosh Today*, May 2, 1988, p. 6.

> *Discussion of SCORES virus, with list of antiviral software on networks (for Macintosh). (List includes Kill Scores, Ferret, Vaccine, Interferon, Virus Detective.)*

Dembart, Lee Attack of the Computer Virus *Discover*, Nov. 1984.

Denning, Dorothy Elizabeth Robling *Cryptography and Data Security* Addison-Wesley Publishing Co., Reading, Mass., 1983.

> *Somewhat technical, but an excellent coverage of the use of encryption.*

[DES 1977] Data Encryption Standard *Federal Information Processing Standards Publication 46* National Bureau of Standards, Washington, D.C., Jan. 1977, p. 4.

Dewdney, A. K. Computer Recreations *Scientific American*, May 1984.

[Dewdney 1985 #1] Dewdney, A. K. Computer Recreations *Scientific American*, Mar. 1985.

[Dewdney 1985 #2] Dewdney, A. K. Computer Recreations *Scientific American*, Sept. 1985.

Dewdney, A. K. Computer Recreations *Scientific American*, Jan. 1987.
> *NOTE: The May 1984, March 1985, and January 1987 Scientific American Computer Recreations columns have been reprinted in* The Armchair Universe, *W. H. Freeman, 1988.*

Dove, Brian Accidentally Formatted Hard Disk can be Salvaged *Input*, Dec. 1986, p. 2G.

[DPMA 1987] Model Computer Crime Act Adopted by DPMA; Provides Guidelines for State, Local Governments *Inside DPMA* Summer 1987, p. 14.
> *A report of the approval of the model computer crime act by the DPMA, and some of the ongoing activities.*

[FIPS 1981] Guidelines for Implementing and Using the NBS Data Encryption Standard *FIPS Publication 74*, U.S. Department of Commerce/National Bureau of Standards, Washington D.C., Apr., 1981.

Fites, Philip. E., Martin P. J. Kratz, and Alan F. Brebner *Control and Security in Computer Information Systems* W. H. Freeman/Computer Science Press, 1988.
> *Specifically intended as a textbook, rather than a "popular press" book, a technical reference, or exposition of one manufacturer's ideas.*

[Florida Virus 1988] Computers Feeling Sickly as "Viruses" Strike Florida *Globe & Mail*, Jan. 13 1988, p. B9.

Gerhard, William D. *Networks of Computers*, National Security Agency Fort George G. Meade, Maryland 20755.

Graham, Gordon Do Your Discs Carry an Invisible Software Virus? *Quill and Quire*, 54, No. 5, May 1988, p. 20.

Howitt, Doran Of Worms and Booby Traps *Infoworld*, Nov. 19, 1984.

[IBM 1984] Good Security Practices for Personal Computers *IBM Data Security Support Programs*, First Edition, Mar. 1984.

IFIP, *Proceedings of Fifth International Conference and Exhibition on Computer Security* Gold Coast, Queensland, Australia, May 1988.

INFOMac Digests are distributed via e-mail systems throughout North America.

Jorgensen, Bud Xmas Card Gives IBM a Computer Holiday in the *Quidnunc* column of the *Globe & Mail* Report on Business Section, Dec. 1987.

A description of clogging IBM's PROFS internal system due to multi-
ple reproductions of a (graphics) Christmas card. Apparently many
people found it very attractive, and "filled up" available e-mail capacity
to the extent that the system shut down for nearly three days.

Kehoe, Louise Concern Rises Over the Recent Spread of Software Viruses
Financial Post June 6, 1988, p. 47.

A fairly rational article discussing recent events. Includes some com-
mon-sense tips to help in avoiding problems.

Kratz, Martin P. J. The Creator and the Benefits of Creation: Protection of
Software in the Information Revolution *Dalhousie Law Journal 555*, 1985, pp. 570-
571.

This is one of the first times someone "blew the whistle" on the possi-
bility of vendors actually spreading diseased software as a means of
copy protection. It's not certain that this paper caused *abandonment*
of this unethical plan, but it is clear that software vendors (or their
legal counsels) abandoned their plans a short time after this paper's
publication.

[Kratz 1986 #1] Kratz, Martin Paul John Computer Abuse by Children *Resource*
News, Legal Resource Centre, Faculty of Extension, University of Alberta, Apr.
1986, p. 18.

Non-technical general-public introduction.

[Kratz 1986 #2] Kratz, Martin P. J. Computer Crime *Resource News*, Legal
Resource Centre, Faculty of Extension, University of Alberta, Apr. 1986, p. 9.

Nontechnical general-public introduction.

Krauss, Leonard I, and Aileen McGahan *Computer Fraud and Countermeasures*
Prentice-Hall, Englewood Cliffs N. J., 1979.

This book is a classic and contains a great deal of useful information for
the professional in the field of information systems security. Much of it
remains current after a decade or more, especially the material on
motivations and administrative controls.

Landreth, Bill, with Howard Rheingold *Out of the Inner Circle: A Hacker's Guide to*
Computer Security Microsoft Press, Bellevue, Washington 1987 (distributed by
Simon & Schuster).

This is written from the perspective of the hacker or perpetrator; it can
be rather frightening at times.

Lobel, J. *Foiling the System Breakers: Computer Security and Access Control* McGraw-
Hill, 1986.

One of the best references. There is a bias toward Honeywell approaches, but it is limited and mostly confined to specific sections.

Madsen, C. W. The World Meganetwork and Terrorism *Proceedings of the IFIP Conference and Exhibition on Computer Security*, May 1988.

A paper outlining the degree of connectivity that is growing in worldwide communications networks. Considers vulnerabilities in infrastructure and support components such as power supplies, switching nodes, as well as data exposures.

McCain, Mark Electronic Terrorists Prey on Computer Users Who Link Up with "Bulletin Boards" by Phone *Globe & Mail* Report on Business, May 26, 1987, p. B15.

A description of some of the events and methods presenting risk to users of public domain software.

Mersich, Dan Too Smart by Half *Canadian Datasystems* Sept. 1986, p. 24.

Discussion of problem of supplier of material using copy protection methods (worms) that will harm purchaser and potential liability arising.

Miller, James E Characteristics of the Computer Environment That Provide Opportunities For Crime *Computer Security* IFIP, 1984.

Murphy, Jamie A Threat from Malicious Software *Time*, Nov. 4, 1985.

[NASA 1987] West German Hackers Break into NASA System *Globe & Mail* Sept. 16, 1987, pp. 1ff.

Report of group of hackers penetrating NASA computer network.

[Newspaper Virus 1988] Disk "Virus" Infests Newspaper *Edmonton Journal*, May 17, 1988, p. C3.

Description of virus in Providence Journal-Bulletin newspaper systems. May have corrupted CHKDSK program and spread when people were checking for problem files. According to report, trigger mechanism unknown, initial infection source unknown.

O'Connor, Rory Apple's Rx: Virus Fix, New Systems *Macintosh Today*, May 2, 1988, pp. 1, 7.

Report of Apple's work on the virus problem. (Probably the interest in viruses took on urgency with MacMag's virus.)

Parker, Donn B. *Crime by Computer* Charles Scribner's Sons, New York, 1976.

Parker, Donn B. *Ethical Conflicts in Computer Science and Technology* AFIPS Press, Arlington, Va.

Parker, Donn B. *Fighting Computer Crime* Charles Scribner & Sons, N. Y., 1983.

[Peace Virus 1988] Montrealer Spread Virus *Globe & Mail* Mar. 17, 1988, p. B19.
> *Early report of deliberate spread of (harmless) virus by MacMag pub-*
> *lisher. Also covered in CBC* Morningside *interview April 15, 1988.*
> *Interview notes that method of propagation was simply to leave on a*
> *computer in a store for two days; estimated 350,000 people worldwide*
> *saw the "peace message" on March 2, 1988. Also said to have been in*
> *Aldus software, making it the first reported instance in commercial*
> *software.*

[PLO 1988] Saboteur Uses "Virus" to Kill Computer Files in Israel *Edmonton Journal* Jan. 8, 1988, p. A9.
> *Report of someone placing a "virus" in files in Hebrew University in*
> *Jerusalem. Also known as the PLO virus.*

Podell, Harold J. and Marshall D. Abrams A Computer Security Glossary for the Advanced Practitioner *Computer Security Journal* IV, No. 1, 1987.
> *This glossary is somewhat technical and oriented toward U.S. gov-*
> *ernment terminology.*

Pozzo, Maria M., and Terence E. Gray Computer Virus Containment in Untrusted Computing Environments *Information Security: The Challenge* Preprints of papers from the fourth IFIP Security of Information Systems Conference, Monte-Carlo, Dec. 1986.
> *This paper is somewhat technical. It discusses issues involving the use*
> *of encryption and other methods to limit the spread of viruses in vari-*
> *ous computing environments.*

[RCMP #1] Security in the EDP Environment *RCMP Security Information Publications No. 1*, 2nd ed., Oct. 1981.

[RCMP #2] EDP Threat Assessments: Concepts and Planning Guide *RCMP Security Information Publications No. 2*, Jan. 1982.

[RCMP #3] Target Hardening *RCMP Security Information Publications No. 3*, Sept. 1983.
> *This volume of the RCMP series concentrates mostly on physical secu-*
> *rity: keeping people off the premises. There are some good pointers*
> *about the stages of response, using different methods in rings of*
> *protection to make penetration difficult, and so on; virtually nothing*
> *on non-physical methods.*

[RCMP 1987] Small Computer Systems Security and Small Systems Questionnaire *EDP Security Bulletin*, Royal Canadian Mounted Police "T" Directorate, 12 No. 1, Jul. 1987, pp. 4-7.

> *The questionnaire is not copyrighted and may be reproduced for use; it comes in French and English.*

[Rubenking 1988 #1] Rubenking, Neil J. Antivirus Programs Fight Data Loss *PC Magazine*, June 28, 1988, p. 36.

> *Short review of several antivirus programs with comments on effectiveness, contact information.*

[Rubenking 1988 #2] Rubenking, Neil J. How Vaccine Programs Work *PC Magazine*, June 28, 1988, p. 35.

> *Very short box outlining major areas of interest in preventing virus damage.*

Safeware Insurance Company Theft, Power Surges Are Major Causes of PC Losses report by Safeware Insurance Company of 1987 survey.

> *Identifies power surges (often through modems), theft as primary loss causes, with dollar figures for 1987. See also 1986 survey.*

Serviss, Shirley Computers and the Law *Resource News 10*, No. 8, Apr. 1986.

Seymour, Jim, and Jonathan Matzkin Confronting the Growing Threat of Harmful Computer Software Viruses *PC Magazine*, June 28, 1988, p. 33.

> *Article describing what a virus is, how it works, and frequent transmission means. Well-known recent instances are mentioned.*

Shapiro, Neil L. Viral Infection *MacUser Magazine* 4, No. 5, May 1988, p. 23.

Sheehy, Therese Twelve States Add Computer Crime Law During 1984 *Data Management Magazine* Legislative Report, Oct. 1984.

Sookman, Barry Electronic Information: The Liability of Providers *Computing Canada*, Sept. 17, 1987, pp. 12, 26.

> *A discussion of the liability of providers to ensure accuracy and legality (not hate literature, for instance) of information on their databases.*

Stieren, Carl Devilishly Clever Viruses May Be Lurking to Devour Computer Data *Globe & Mail* Mar. 7, 1988, p. C15.

> *A brief description of what a virus does and how it gets into systems, with some helpful nontechnical hints for avoiding viruses.*

Thornton, Mary "Hackers" Ignore Consequences of Their High-Tech Joy Rides *The Washington Post* May 2, 1984.

[Time 1985] A Threat from Malicious Software *Time*, Nov. 4, 1985.

[Time Life 1986] *Computer Security*, Time Life Books, Alexandria, Virginia, 1986.
Very readable treatment of the issues of computer security. The level of technical detail is not deep; highly recommended as an introduction.

[Virus 1988] "Virus" Leads to Indictment *Globe & Mail* May 31, 1988, p. B23.
Security officer in Fort Worth is fired, uses knowledge of access codes and system to delete 160,000 files from former employer's computer. The reported actions of accessing the system, probably through a trapdoor, then deleting files and erasing activity logs, need not have involved a virus.

Wyles, John Companies Blamed for Scope of Italy's Computer Piracy *Financial Post*, June 6, 1988, p. 46.
Report suggesting that piracy of software is endemic in Italy, and seriously damaging the indigenous software industry. Suggests that the worst of the problem is perpetrated by companies rather than individuals.

INDEX

H4